Scriptural Rosary based on God's Promises

Experience the Power of God's Word Combined with the Rosary

Over 1500 Promises to Meditate

CHARLES MICHAEL

GIFTED BOOKS AND MEDIA

Scripture quotations are from Douay-Rheims 1899 American Edition Version (public domain) and from Catholic Public Domain Version. (Public domain).

Compiled by Charles Michael

Printed in the United States of America

Paperback ISBN: 978-1-947343-18-4

Published by Jayclad Publishing LLC

Gifted Books and Media
www.giftedbookstore.com

Table of Contents

How to Pray the Scriptural Rosary

1. Make the Sign of the Cross
2. Say the "Apostles' Creed"
3. Say the "Our Father"
4. Say three "Hail Marys" for Faith, Hope, and love
5. Say the "Glory Be"
6. Announce the First Mystery
7. Say the "Our Father"
8. Read the Scripture verse before each Hail Mary (ten verses and ten "Hail Marys" per decade)
9. Say the "Glory Be"
10. Say the "O My Jesus" prayer
11. Announce the Next Mystery; and repeat the above steps (7-10).
12. Say the closing prayers (Hail Holy Queen, etc.)
13. Make the "Sign of the Cross"

The Joyful Mysteries

Decade 1 (The Annunciation)

Our Father…

In the sixth month, the Angel Gabriel was sent by God, to a city of Galilee named Nazareth, to a virgin betrothed to a man whose name was Joseph, of the house of David; and the name of the virgin was Mary. (Luk 1:26-27)
Hail Mary...

Upon entering, the Angel said to her: "Hail, full of grace. The Lord is with you. Blessed are you among women." (Luk 1:28)
Hail Mary...

When she had heard this, she was disturbed by his words, and she considered what kind of greeting this might be. (Luk 1:29)
Hail Mary...

The Angel said to her: "Do not be afraid, Mary, for you have found favor with God." (Luk 1:30)
Hail Mary...

Behold, you shall conceive in your womb, and you shall bear a son, and you shall call his name Jesus. (Luk 1:31)
Hail Mary...

He will be great, and he will be called the Son of the Most High, and the Lord God will give him the throne of David his father. And he will reign in the house of Jacob for eternity. And his kingdom shall have no end. (Luk 1:32-33)
Hail Mary...

Then Mary said to the Angel, "How shall this be, since I am a virgin?" (Luk 1:34)
Hail Mary...

The angel said to her: "The Holy Spirit will come upon you, and the power of the Most High will overshadow you." (Luk 1:35)
Hail Mary...

Because of this, the child who will be born will be holy and he shall be called the Son of God. (Luk 1:35)
Hail Mary...

Then Mary said: "Behold, I am the handmaid of the Lord. Let it be done to me according to your word." And the Angel departed from her. (Luk 1:38)
Hail Mary...

Glory Be…

Decade 2 (The Visitation)

Our Father…

In those days, Mary, rising up, traveled quickly into the hill country, to a city of Judah. And she entered into the house of Zechariah, and she greeted Elizabeth. (Luk 1:39-40)
Hail Mary...

As Elizabeth heard the greeting of Mary, the baby leaped in her womb, and Elizabeth was filled with the Holy Spirit. (Luk 1:41)
Hail Mary...

Elizabeth was filled with the Holy Spirit. And she cried out with a loud voice and said: "Blessed are you among women, and blessed is the fruit of your womb." (Luk 1:41-42)
Hail Mary...

Blessed are you who believed, for the things that were spoken to you by the Lord shall be accomplished. (Luk 1:45)
Hail Mary...

Mary said: "My soul magnifies the Lord." (Luk 1:46)
Hail Mary

My spirit leaps for joy in God my Savior. (Luk 1:47)
Hail Mary...

He has looked with favor on the humility of his handmaid. (Luk 1:48)
Hail Mary...

Behold, from this time, all generations shall call me blessed. (Luk 1:48)
Hail Mary...

He has accomplished powerful deeds with his arm. He has scattered the proud in the intentions of their heart. (Luk 1:51)
Hail Mary...

He has filled the hungry with good things, and the rich he has sent away empty. (Luk 1:53)
Hail Mary...

Glory Be…

Decade 3 (The Nativity)

Our Father…

While they were in Bethlehem, the time came for her to have her baby. (Luk 2:6)
Hail Mary...

She brought forth her firstborn son. And she wrapped him in swaddling clothes. (Luk 2:7)
Hail Mary...

She wrapped him in swaddling clothes and laid him in a manger, because there was no room for them at the inn. (Luk 2:7)
Hail Mary...

There were shepherds in that region, keeping watch in the night over their flock. An Angel of the Lord stood near them, and the glory of God shone around them, and they were struck with a great fear. (Luk 2:8-9)
Hail Mary...

The Angel said to them: "Do not be afraid. For, behold, I proclaim to you good news of great joy, which will be for all the people. (Luk 2:10)
Hail Mary...

For today a Savior has been born for you in the city of David: he is the Messiah, the Lord. (Luk 2:11)
Hail Mary...

Glory to God in the highest, and on earth peace to those whom he favors. (Luk 2:14)
Hail Mary...

When the Angels had departed from them into heaven, the shepherds said to one another, "Let us go to Bethlehem and see this thing, which has happened, which the Lord has revealed to us." (Luk 2:15)
Hail Mary...

When Jesus had been born in Bethlehem of Judah, in the days of king Herod, behold, Magi from the east arrived in Jerusalem. (Matt 2:1)
Hail Mary...

Entering the home, they found the boy with his mother Mary. And so, falling prostrate, they adored him. And opening their treasures, they offered him gifts: gold, frankincense, and myrrh. (Matt 2:11)
Hail Mary...

Glory Be…

Decade 4 (The Presentation)

Our Father…

After the days of their purification were fulfilled, according to the law of Moses, they brought him to Jerusalem, in order to present him to the Lord. (Luk 2:22)
Hail Mary...

There was a man in Jerusalem, whose name was Simeon, and this man was righteous and God-fearing, awaiting the consolation of Israel. And the Holy Spirit was upon him. (Luk 2:25)
Hail Mary...

The Holy Spirit was with him and had assured him that he would not die before he had seen the Lord's promised Messiah. (Luk 2:25-26)
Hail Mary...

He went to the temple, guided by the Holy Spirit. And when the child Jesus was brought in by his parents, in order to do for him according to the custom of the law, Simeon took him up, into his arms, and he praised God. (Luk 2:27-28)
Hail Mary...

Now you may dismiss your servant in peace, O Lord, according to your word. (Luk 2:29)
Hail Mary...

My eyes have seen your salvation, which you have prepared before the face of all peoples. (Luk 2:30-31)
Hail Mary...

The light of revelation to the nations and the glory of your people Israel. (Luk 2:32)
Hail Mary...

Simeon blessed them, and he said to his mother Mary: "Behold, this child has been set for the ruin and for the salvation of many in Israel, and as a sign from God which will be contradicted. (Luk 2:34)
Hail Mary...

After they had performed all things according to the law of the Lord, they returned to Galilee, to their city, Nazareth. (Luk 2:39)
Hail Mary...

The child grew, and he was strengthened with the fullness of wisdom. And the grace of God was in him. (Luk 2:40)
Hail Mary...

Glory Be…

Decade 5 (The Finding of the Child Jesus in the temple)

Our Father…

The parents of Jesus went every year to Jerusalem, at the time of the feast of Passover. And when he had become twelve years old, they went to Jerusalem, according to the custom of the feast day. (Luk 2:41-42)
Hail Mary...

Having completed the days, when they returned, the boy Jesus remained in Jerusalem. And his parents did not realize this. (Luk 2:43)
Hail Mary...

Supposing that he was in the company, they went a day's journey, seeking him among their relatives and acquaintances. And not finding him, they returned to Jerusalem, seeking him. (Luk 2:44-45)
Hail Mary...

After three days, they found him in the temple, sitting in the midst of the teachers, listening to them and asking them questions. (Luk 2:46)
Hail Mary...

All who listened to him were astonished over his wisdom and his responses. (Luk 2:47)
Hail Mary...

Upon seeing him, they wondered. And his mother said to him: "Son, why have you acted this way toward us? Behold, your father and I were searching for you in great anxiety." (Luk 2:48)
Hail Mary...

He said to them: "Why were you looking for me? Did you not know that I must be in my Father's house?" (Luk 2:49)
Hail Mary...

They did not understand the word that he spoke to them. (Luk 2:50)
Hail Mary...

He went with them and came to Nazareth. And he was obedient to them. And his mother kept all these things in her heart. (Luk 2:51)
Hail Mary...

Jesus advanced in wisdom, and in age, and in grace, with God and men. (Luk 2:52)
Hail Mary...

Glory Be…

The Sorrowful Mysteries

Decade 1 (The Agony in the Garden)

Our Father...

Then Jesus went with them to a garden, which is called Gethsemani. And he said to his disciples, "Sit down here, while I go there and pray." (Matt 26:36)
Hail Mary...

Taking with him Peter and the two sons of Zebedee, he began to be sorrowful and saddened. (Matt 26:37)
Hail Mary...

He said to them: "My soul is sorrowful, even unto death. Stay here and keep vigil with me." (Matt 26:38)
Hail Mary...

Continuing on a little further, he fell prostrate on his face, praying and saying: "My Father, if it is possible, let this chalice pass away from me. Yet, not as I will, but as you will." (Matt 26:39)
Hail Mary...

Again, a second time, he went and prayed, saying, "My Father, if this chalice cannot pass away, unless I drink it, let your will be done." (Matt 26:42)
Hail Mary...

Again, he went and found them sleeping, for their eyes were heavy. (Matt 26:43)
Hail Mary...

Leaving them behind, again he went and prayed for the third time, saying the same words. (Matt 26:44)
Hail Mary...

Then he approached his disciples and said to them: "Are you still sleeping and resting?. Behold, the hour is at hand, and the Son of man will be betrayed into the hands of sinners." (Matt 26:45)
Hail Mary...

Rise up; let us go. Behold, he who will betray me draws near. (Matt 26:46)
Hail Mary...

While he was still speaking, behold, Judas, one of the twelve, arrived, and with him was a large crowd with swords and clubs, sent from the leaders of the priests and the elders of the people. (Matt 26:47)

Hail Mary...

Glory Be…

Decade 2 (The Scourging at the Pillar)

Our Father…

Immediately in the morning, after the leaders of the priests had taken counsel with the elders and the scribes and the entire council, binding Jesus, they led him away and delivered him to Pilate. (Mrk 15:1-2)
Hail Mary...

Pilate went outside to them, and he said, "What accusation are you bringing against this man?" (Jn 18:29)
Hail Mary...

They responded and said to him, "If he were not an evil-doer, we would not have handed him over to you." (Jn 18:30)
Hail Mary...

Therefore, Pilate said to them, "Take him yourselves and judge him according to your own law." Then the Jews said to him, "It is not lawful for us to execute anyone." (Jn 18:31)
Hail Mary...

Then Pilate entered the praetorium again, and he called Jesus and said to him, "You are the king of the Jews?" (Jn 18:33)
Hail Mary...

Jesus responded, "Are you saying this of yourself, or have others spoken to you about me?" (Jn 18:34)
Hail Mary...

Pilate responded: "Am I a Jew? Your own nation and the high priests have handed you over to me. What have you done?" (Jn 18:35)
Hail Mary...

My kingdom is not of this world. If my kingdom were of this world, my followers would certainly fight to keep me from being handed over to the Jews. But my kingdom is not from here.
Hail Mary...

Pilate said to him, "You are a king, then?" Jesus answered, "You are saying that I am a king. For this I was born, and for this I came into the world: so that I may offer testimony to the truth. Everyone who is of the truth hears my voice." Pilate said to him, "What is truth?" And when he had said this,

he went out again to the Jews, and he said to them, "I find no case against him. (Jn 18:37-38)
Hail Mary...

Pilate then took Jesus into custody and scourged him. (Jn 19:1)
Hail Mary...

Glory Be…

Decade 3 (The Crowning with Thorns)

Our Father…

Then the soldiers led him away to the court of the praetorium. And they called together the entire cohort. (Mrk 15:16)
Hail Mary...

They clothed him in a purple robe. And made a crown of thorns and placed it on him. (Mrk 15:17)
Hail Mary...

They stripped him and put a scarlet cloak around him. They plaited a crown of thorns and placed it on his head. (Matt 27:28-29)
Hail Mary...

They placed a reed in his right hand and knelt before him, and they mocked him, saying, "Hail, King of the Jews." (Matt 27:29)
Hail Mary...

Spitting on him, they took the reed and struck his head. (Matt 27:30)
Hail Mary...

They began to salute him: "Hail, king of the Jews." (Mrk 15:18)
Hail Mary...

They struck his head with a reed, and they spit on him. And kneeling down, they reverenced him. (Mrk 15:19)
Hail Mary...

Then Pilate went outside again, and he said to them: "Behold, I am bringing him out to you, so that you may realize that I find no case against him." (Then Jesus went out, bearing the crown of thorns and the purple garment.) And he said to them, "Behold the man." (Jn 19:4-5)
Hail Mary...

But they were crying out: "Take him away! Take him away! Crucify him!" (Jn 19:15)
Hail Mary...

Pilate said to them, "Shall I crucify your king?" The high priests responded, "We have no king except Caesar." (Jn 19:15)
Hail Mary...

Glory Be...

Decade 4 (The Carrying of the Cross)

Our Father...

If anyone is willing to come after me: let him deny himself, and take up his cross every day, and follow me. (Luk 9:23)
Hail Mary...

Whoever will have saved his life, will lose it. Yet whoever will have lost his life for my sake, will save it. (Luk 9:24)
Hail Mary...

He then handed him over to them to be crucified. And they took Jesus and led him away. (Jn 19:16)
Hail Mary...

After they had mocked him, they stripped him of the purple, and they clothed him in his own garments. And they led him away, so that they might crucify him. (Mrk 15:20)
Hail Mary...

Carrying his own cross, he went forth to the place which is called Calvary, but in Hebrew it is called the Place of the Skull. (Jn 19:17)
Hail Mary...

They compelled a certain passerby, Simon the Cyrenian, who was arriving from the countryside, the father of Alexander and Rufus, to take up his cross. (Mrk 15:21)
Hail Mary...

Then a great crowd of people followed him, with women who were mourning and lamenting him. (Luk 23:27)
Hail Mary...

But Jesus, turning to them, said: "Daughters of Jerusalem, do not weep over me. Instead, weep over yourselves and over your children." (Luk 23:28)
Hail Mary...

Behold, the days will arrive in which they will say, 'Blessed are the barren, and the wombs that have not borne, and the breasts that have not nursed.' (Luk 23:29)
Hail Mary...

They led him through to the place called Golgotha, which means, 'the Place of Calvary.' And they gave him wine with myrrh to drink. But he did not accept it. (Mrk 15:22-23)
Hail Mary...

Glory Be…

Decade 5 (The Crucifixion)
Our Father…

When they arrived at the place that is called Calvary, they crucified him there, with the robbers, one to the right and the other to the left. (Luk 23:33)
Hail Mary...

Jesus said, "Father, forgive them, for they know not what they do." And they cast lots to divide his garments. (Luk 23:34)
Hail Mary...

The passersby blasphemed him, shaking their heads and saying, "Ah, you who would destroy the temple of God, and in three days rebuild it, save yourself by descending from the cross." (Mrk 15:29-30)
Hail Mary...

One of those robbers who were hanging blasphemed him, saying, "If you are the Christ, save yourself and us." (Luk 23:39)
Hail Mary...

But the other responded by rebuking him, saying: "Do you have no fear of God, since you are under the same condemnation?" (Luk 23:40)
Hail Mary...

Jesus said to him, "Amen I say to you, this day you shall be with me in Paradise." (Luk 23:43)
Hail Mary...

Standing beside the cross of Jesus were his mother, and his mother's sister, and Mary of Cleophas, and Mary Magdalene. Therefore, when Jesus had seen his mother and the disciple whom he loved standing near, he said to his mother, "Woman, behold your son." (Jn 19:25-26)
Hail Mary...

It was nearly noon, and a darkness occurred over the entire earth, until three in the afternoon. (Luk 23:44)
Hail Mary...

Then Jesus, crying out again with a loud voice, gave up his life. (Matt 27:50)
Hail Mary...

Behold, the veil of the temple was torn into two parts, from top to bottom. And the earth was shaken, and the rocks were split apart. (Matt 27:51)
Hail Mary...

Glory Be…

The Glorious Mysteries

Decade 1 (The Resurrection of our Lord)

Our Father…

Therefore, you also, indeed, have sorrow now. But I will see you again, and your heart shall rejoice. And no one will take away your joy from you. (Jn 16:22)
Hail Mary...

Then, on the first day of the week, early in the morning, they went to the tomb, carrying the aromatic spices that they had prepared. (Luk 24:1)
Hail Mary...

Behold, a great earthquake occurred. For an Angel of the Lord descended from heaven, and as he approached, he rolled back the stone and sat down on it. (Matt 28:2)
Hail Mary...

Then the Angel responded by saying to the women: "Do not be afraid. For I know that you are seeking Jesus, who was crucified. He is not here. For he has risen, just as he said. Come and see the place where the Lord was placed." (Matt 28:5-6)
Hail Mary...

He is not here, for he has risen. Recall how he spoke to you, when he was still in Galilee, saying: 'For the Son of man must be delivered into the hands of sinful men, and be crucified, and on the third day rise again.' (Luk 24:6-7)
Hail Mary...

Go quickly and tell his disciples that he has risen. And behold, he is going ahead of you to Galilee. There you shall see him. (Matt 28:7)
Hail Mary...

They went out of the tomb quickly, with fear and in great joy, running to announce it to his disciples. (Matt 28:8)
Hail Mary...

And behold, Jesus met them on their way and greeted them. But they drew near and took hold of his feet, and they worshipped him. (Matt 28:9)
Hail Mary...

Then Jesus said to them: "Do not be afraid. Go, announce it to my brothers, so that they may go to Galilee. There they shall see me." (Matt 28:10)
Hail Mary...

After his suffering, he also presented himself alive to them by many proofs, appearing to them throughout forty days and speaking about the kingdom of God. (Acts 1:3)
Hail Mary...

Glory Be...

Decade 2 (The Ascension)

Our Father...

Then he led them out as far as Bethania. And lifting up his hands, he blessed them. (Luk 24:50)
Hail Mary...

Jesus, drawing near, spoke to them, saying: "All authority has been given to me in heaven and on earth." (Matt 28:18)
Hail Mary...

Therefore, go forth and teach all nations, baptizing them in the name of the Father and of the Son and of the Holy Spirit. (Matt 28:19)
Hail Mary...

Teach them to observe all that I have ever commanded you. (Matt 28:20)
Hail Mary...

I am with you always, even to the end of the age. (Matt 28:20)
Hail Mary...

It happened that, while he was blessing them, he withdrew from them, and he was carried up into heaven. (Luk 24:51)
Hail Mary...

Indeed, the Lord Jesus, after he had spoken to them, was taken up into heaven, and he sits at the right hand of God. (Mrk 16:19)
Hail Mary...

They worshiped him and they returned to Jerusalem with great joy. (Luk 24:52)
Hail Mary...

They were always in the temple, praising and blessing God. (Luk 24:53)
Hail Mary...

They went forth, and preached the good news everywhere, the Lord worked with them, and confirmed the word with signs that accompanied it. (Mrk 16:20)
Hail Mary...

Glory Be...

Decade 3 (The Coming of the Holy Spirit)

Our Father...

I am sending the Promise of my Father upon you. But you must stay in the city, until such time as you are clothed with power from on high. (Luk 24:49)
Hail Mary...

And staying with them, he instructed them that they should not depart from Jerusalem, but that they should wait for the Promise of the Father, "about which you have heard from me," he said, For John, indeed, baptized with water, but you shall be baptized with the Holy Spirit, not many days from now." (Acts 1:4-5)
Hail Mary...

When they had entered the city, they went upstairs to the room where Peter and John, James and Andrew, Philip and Thomas, Bartholomew and Matthew, James of Alphaeus and Simon the Zealot, and Jude of James, were staying. (Acts 1:13)
Hail Mary...

When the days of Pentecost were completed, they were all together in the same place. And suddenly, there came a sound from heaven, like that of a wind approaching violently, and it filled the entire house where they were sitting. (Acts 2:1-2)
Hail Mary...

There appeared to them divided tongues, as if of fire, and a tongue rested upon each one of them. (Acts 2:3)
Hail Mary...

They were all filled with the Holy Spirit. And they began to speak in various languages, just as the Holy Spirit gave them ability. (Acts 2:4)
Hail Mary...

When this sound occurred, the multitude came together and was confused in mind, because each one was listening to them speaking in his own language. (Acts 2:6)
Hail Mary...

Therefore, being exalted to the right hand of God, and having received from the Father the Promise of the Holy Spirit, he poured this out, just as you now see and hear. (Acts 2:33)
Hail Mary...

I will pour out my spirit upon all flesh, and your sons and your daughters will prophesy; your elders will dream dreams, and your youths will see visions. (Joel 2:28)
Hail Mary...

In those days I will pour out my spirit upon my servants and handmaids. And I will grant wonders in the sky and on earth: blood and fire and the vapor of smoke. (Joel 2:29-30)
Hail Mary...

Glory Be...

Decade 4 (The Assumption of the Blessed Virgin Mary)
Our Father...

The temple of God was opened in heaven. And the Ark of his covenant was seen in his temple. And there were flashes of lightnings and noises, and thunders, and an earthquake, and great hail. (Rev 11:19)
Hail Mary...

Great sign appeared in heaven: a woman clothed with the sun, and the moon was under her feet, and on her head was a crown of twelve stars. (Rev 12:1)
Hail Mary...

She was with child, and the pains and suffering of childbirth made her cry out. (Rev 12:2)
Hail Mary...

After the dragon saw that he had been thrown down to the earth, he pursued the woman who brought forth the male child. (Rev 12:13)
Hail Mary...

The two wings of a great eagle were given to the woman, so that she might fly away from the serpent, into the wilderness, to her place, where she is nourished for a time, and times, and half a time. (Rev 12:14)
Hail Mary...

The dragon was angry at the woman. And so he went away to do battle with the remainder of her offspring, those who keep the commandments of God and who hold to the testimony of Jesus Christ. (Rev 12:17)
Hail Mary...

The prayer of one who humbles himself will pierce the clouds. And it will not be consoled until it draws near; and it will not withdraw until the Most High beholds. (Sir 35:21)
Hail Mary...

Be humbled under the powerful hand of God, so that he may exalt you in the time of visitation. (1 Pet 5:6)
Hail Mary...

God resists the proud, but he gives grace to the humble. (Jas 4:6)
Hail Mary...

Seek the Lord, all you humble of the earth; you who obey his commands. Seek righteousness and humble yourselves before the Lord. Perhaps, you might be hidden in the day of the fury of the Lord. (Zeph 2:30
Hail Mary...

Glory Be...

Decade 5 (The Coronation of the Blessed Mother)

Our Father...

He who is mighty has done great things for me, and holy is his name. (Luk 1:49)
Hail Mary...

O daughter, you have been blessed by the Lord, the most high God, above all the women on earth. (Judith 13:18)
Hail Mary...

All these were constantly devoting themselves in prayer with the women, including Mary, the mother of Jesus, and with his brothers. (Acts 1:14)
Hail Mary...

Through the heart of the mercy of our God, by which, descending from on high, he has visited us, to illuminate those who sit in darkness and in the shadow of death, and to direct our feet in the way of peace. (Luk 1:78-79)
Hail Mary...

It happened that, when he was saying these things, a certain woman from the crowd, lifting up her voice, said to him, "Blessed is the womb that bore you and the breasts that nursed you." (Luk 11:27)
Hail Mary...

They will remember your name always, for generation after generation. Because of this, people will praise you forever and ever. (Ps 45:17)
Hail Mary...

When Jesus had seen his mother and the disciple whom he loved standing near, he said to his mother, "Woman, behold your son." Next, he said to the disciple, "Behold your mother." And from that hour, the disciple accepted her as his own. (Jn 19:26-27)

Hail Mary...

Obedience is better than sacrifice. And to heed is greater than to offer the fat of rams. (1 Sam 15:22)
Hail Mary...

Blessed are those who preserve my ways. Listen to discipline, and become wise, and do not be willing to cast it aside. (Pro 8:32-33)
Hail Mary...

Whoever listens to me will not be put to shame, and whoever works with me will not sin. (Sir 24:22)
Hail Mary...

Glory Be...

The Luminous Mysteries

Decade 1 (The Baptism of our Lord)

Our Father…

I baptize you with water for repentance, but he who will come after me is more powerful than me. I am not worthy to carry his shoes. He will baptize you with the fire of the Holy Spirit. (Matt 3:11)
Hail Mary...

This is the one about whom I said, "After me comes a man, who is greater than me, because he was before me." (Jn 1:30)
Hail Mary...

I myself did not know him. Yet it is for this reason that I come baptizing with water: so that he may be revealed to Israel. (Jn 1:31)
Hail Mary...

Jesus came from Galilee, to John at the Jordan, in order to be baptized by him. (Matt 3:13)
Hail Mary...

John tried to prevent him, saying, "I ought to be baptized by you, and yet you have come to me?" (Matt 3:14)
Hail Mary...

Jesus said to him: "Let it be so now. For in this way it is fitting for us to fulfill all righteousness." Then John agreed. (Jn 3:15)
Hail Mary...

Jesus, having been baptized, ascended from the water immediately, and behold, the heavens were opened to him. And he saw the Spirit of God descending like a dove and alighting on him. (Matt 3:16)
Hail Mary...

Behold, there was a voice from heaven, saying: "This is my beloved Son, in whom I am well pleased." (Matt 3:17)
Hail Mary...

John offered testimony, saying: "For I saw the Spirit descending from heaven like a dove; and he remained upon him." (Jn 1:32)
Hail Mary...

I did not know him. But he who sent me to baptize with water said to me: 'He over whom you will see the Spirit descending and remaining upon him, this is the one who baptizes with the Holy Spirit.' (Jn 1:33)
Hail Mary...

Glory Be...

Decade 2 (The Wedding at Cana)

Our Father...

On the third day, a wedding was held in Cana of Galilee, and the mother of Jesus was there. Now Jesus was also invited to the wedding, with his disciples. (Jn 2:1-2)
Hail Mary...

When the wine had given out, the mother of Jesus said to him, "They have no wine." (Jn 2:3)
Hail Mary...

Jesus said to her: "What is that to me and to you, woman? My hour has not yet arrived." (Jn 2:4)
Hail Mary...

His mother said to the servants, "Do whatever he tells you." (Jn 2:5)
Hail Mary...

Now in that place, there were six stone water jars, for the purification ritual of the Jews, each holding twenty or thirty gallons. (Jn 2:6)
Hail Mary...

Jesus said to them, "Fill the water jars with water." And they filled them to the very top. (Jn 2:7)
Hail Mary...

Jesus said to them, "Now draw from it, and carry it to the chief steward of the feast." And they took it to him. (Jn 2:8)
Hail Mary...

When the chief steward had tasted the water made into wine, since he did not know where it was from, for only the servants who had drawn the water knew, the chief steward called the groom. (Jn 2:9)
Hail Mary...

He said to him: "Everyone offers the good wine first, and then, when they have become drunk, they offer what is inferior. But you have kept the good wine until now." (Jn 2:10)
Hail Mary...

This was the beginning of the signs that Jesus accomplished in Cana of Galilee, and it manifested his glory, and his disciples believed in him. (Jn 2:11)
Hail Mary...

Glory Be…

Decade 3 (The Proclamation of the Kingdom)
Our Father…

The time has been fulfilled and the kingdom of God has drawn near. Repent and believe in the Gospel. (Mrk 1:15)
Hail Mary...

Jesus responded: "Amen, amen, I say to you, unless one has been reborn by water and the Holy Spirit, he is not able to enter into the kingdom of God." (Jn 3:5)
Hail Mary...

From that time, Jesus began to preach, and to say: "Repent. For the kingdom of heaven has drawn near." (Matt 4:17)
Hail Mary...

Jesus traveled throughout all of Galilee, teaching in their synagogues, and preaching the Gospel of the kingdom, and healing every sickness and every infirmity among the people. (Matt 4:23)
Hail Mary...

Going forth, preach, saying: 'For the kingdom of heaven has drawn near.' Cure the infirm, raise the dead, cleanse lepers, cast out demons. You have received freely, so give freely. (Matt 10:7-8)
Hail Mary...

Into whatever city you have entered and they have received you, eat what they set before you. And cure the sick who are in that place, and proclaim to them, 'The kingdom of God has drawn near to you.' (Luk 10:8-9)
Hail Mary...

This good news of the kingdom shall be preached throughout the entire world, as a testimony to all nations. And then the end will occur. (Matt 24:14)
Hail Mary...

It happened afterwards that he was making a journey through the cities and towns, preaching and evangelizing the kingdom of God. And the twelve were with him. (Luk 8:1)
Hail Mary...

When the crowd had realized this, they followed him. And he received them and spoke to them about the kingdom of God. And those who were in need of cures, he healed. (Luk 9:11)
Hail Mary...

Jesus traveled throughout all of the cities and towns, teaching in their synagogues, and preaching the Gospel of the kingdom, and healing every illness and every infirmity. (Matt 9:35)
Hail Mary...

Glory Be...

Decade 4 (The Transfiguration)
Our Father...

After six days, Jesus took Peter and James and his brother John, and he led them onto a lofty mountain separately. (Matt 17:1)
Hail Mary...

He was transfigured before them. And his face shined brightly like the sun. And his garments were made white like snow. (Matt 17:2)
Hail Mary...

Behold, there appeared to them Moses and Elijah, speaking with him. (Matt 17:3)
Hail Mary...

His vestments became radiant and exceedingly white like snow, such as no one on earth is able to whiten them. (Mrk 9:3)
Hail Mary...

Peter responded by saying to Jesus: "Lord, it is good for us to be here.
If you are willing, let us make three tabernacles here, one for you, one for Moses, and one for Elijah." (Matt 17:4)
Hail Mary...

While he was still speaking, behold, a shining cloud overshadowed them. And behold, there was a voice from the cloud, saying: "This is my beloved Son, with whom I am well pleased. Listen to him." (Matt 17:5)
Hail Mary...

The disciples, when they heard the voice, they fell on their faces and were very afraid. (Matt 17:6)
Hail Mary...

Jesus drew near and touched them. And he said to them, "Rise up and do not be afraid." (Matt 17:7)

Hail Mary...

Lifting up their eyes, they saw no one, except Jesus alone. (Matt 17:8)
Hail Mary...

As they were descending from the mountain, Jesus instructed them, saying, "Tell no one about the vision, until the Son of man has risen from the dead." (Matt 17:9)
Hail Mary...

Glory Be...

Decade 5 (The Institution of the Last Supper)

Our Father...

On the first day of Unleavened Bread, the disciples approached Jesus, saying, "Where do you want us to prepare for you to eat the Passover?" (Matt 26:17)
Hail Mary...

Jesus said, "Go into the city, to a certain one, and say to him: 'The Teacher said: My time is near. I am observing the Passover with you, along with my disciples.' "(Matt 26:18)
Hail Mary...

The disciples did just as Jesus appointed to them. And they prepared the Passover. (Matt 26:19)
Hail Mary...

When evening arrived, he sat at table with his twelve disciples. And while they were eating, he said: "Amen I say to you, that one of you is about to betray me." (Matt 26:20-21)
Hail Mary...

Being greatly saddened, each one of them began to say, "Surely, it is not I, Lord?" But he responded by saying: "The one who dips his hand into the bowl with me will betray me. (Matt 26:22-23)
Hail Mary...

Indeed, the Son of man goes, just as it has been written about him. But woe to that man by whom the Son of man will be betrayed. It would be better for that man if he had not been born. (Matt 26:24)
Hail Mary...

While they were eating the meal, Jesus took bread, and he blessed and broke and gave it to his disciples, and he said: "Take and eat. This is my body." (Matt 26:26)
Hail Mary...

Taking the chalice, he gave thanks. And he gave it to them, saying: "Drink from this, all of you." (Matt 26:27)
Hail Mary...

This is my blood of the new covenant, which shall be shed for many for the forgiveness of sins. (Matt 26:28)
Hail Mary...

But I say to you, I will not drink again from this fruit of the vine, until that day when I will drink it new with you in the kingdom of my Father. (Matt 26:29)
Hail Mary...

Glory Be...

Day 1

Decade 1

Our Father…

He blessed them, saying, "Increase and multiply, and fill the waters of the sea: and let the birds be multiplied upon the earth." (Gen 1:22)
Hail Mary...

Let us make man to our image and likeness, and let him have dominion over the fish of the sea, and the birds of the air, and the beasts, and the whole earth, and every creeping creature that moves upon the earth. (Gen 1:26)
Hail Mary...

God blessed them, saying "Increase and multiply, and fill the earth, and subdue it, and rule over the fish of the sea, and the birds of the air, and all living creatures that move upon the earth." (Gen 1:28)
Hail Mary...

God saw all the things that he had made, and they were very good. (Gen 1:31)
Hail Mary...

I will put enmity between you and the woman, between your offspring and her offspring: He shall crush your head, and you will strike his heel. (Gen 3:15)
Hail Mary...

If you do well, will you not be accepted? but if you do badly, will not sin be present at the door? Its desire is for you, but you must master it. (Gen 4:7)
Hail Mary...

God blessed Noah and his sons. And he said to them: "Increase, and multiply, and fill the earth." (Gen 9:1)
Hail Mary...

I will establish my covenant with you, and no longer will all that is flesh be put to death by the waters of a great flood, and, henceforth, there will not be a great flood to utterly destroy the earth. (Gen 9:11)
Hail Mary...

All the land that you see, I will give to you, and to your offspring even forever. And I will make your offspring like the dust of the earth. If any man

is able to number the dust of the earth, he will be able to number your offspring as well. (Gen 13:15-16)
Hail Mary...

The word of the Lord came to Abram by a vision, saying: "Do not be afraid, Abram, I am your protector, and your reward shall be very great." (Gen 15:1)
Hail Mary...

Glory Be…

Decade 2

Our Father…

He brought him outside, and he said to him, "Look toward heaven and count the stars, if you can." And he said to him, "So also will your offspring be." (Gen 15:5)
Hail Mary...

When the sun had set, there came a dark mist, and there appeared a smoking furnace and a lamp of fire passing between those divisions. On that day, God formed a covenant with Abram, saying: "To your offspring I will give this land, from the river of Egypt, even to the great river Euphrates. (Gen 15:17-18)
Hail Mary...

He said to him: "I am the Almighty God. Walk in my sight and become complete. And I will set my covenant between me and you. And I will multiply you very exceedingly." (Gen 17:1-2)
Hail Mary...

God said to him: "As for me, my covenant is with you, and you will be the father of many nations. No longer will your name be called Abram. But you will be called Abraham, for I have established you as the father of many nations." (Gen 17:4-5)
Hail Mary...

He called the name of that place: 'The Lord provides.' Thus, even to this day, it is said: 'On the mountain, the Lord will provide.' (Gen 22:14)
Hail Mary...

'The Lord,' he said, 'in whose sight I walk, will send his Angel with you, and he will direct your way. (Gen 24:40)
Hail Mary...

I will multiply your offspring like the stars of heaven. And I will give to your posterity all these regions. And in your offspring all the nations of the earth

will be blessed, because Abraham obeyed my voice, and kept my precepts and commandments, and observed the ceremonies and the laws. (Gen 26:4-5)
Hail Mary...

I am the God of Abraham your father. Do not be afraid, for I am with you. I will bless you, and I will multiply your offspring because of my servant Abraham. (Gen 26:24)
Hail Mary...

May God almighty bless you, and may he cause you to increase and also to multiply, so that you may be influential among the people. (Gen 28:3)
Hail Mary...

May he give the blessings of Abraham to you, and to your offspring after you, so that you may possess the land where you now live as an alien (Gen 28:4)
Hail Mary...

Glory Be...

Decade 3

Our Father...

Your offspring will be like the dust of the earth. You will spread abroad to the West, and to the East, and to the North, and to the Meridian. And in you and in your offspring, all the tribes of the earth shall be blessed. (Gen 28:14)
Hail Mary...

I will not leave you, until I have done that which I have promised you. (Gen 28:15)
Hail Mary...

I will increase and multiply you, and I will make you influential among the people. And I will give this land to you, and to your offspring after you, as an everlasting possession. (Gen 48:3-4)
Hail Mary...

The scepter from Judah shall not depart, nor the leader's staff from between his feet will be taken away, until he who will be sent arrives, and he will be the expectation of Gentiles. (Gen 49:10)
Hail Mary...

The blood will be for you as a sign in the buildings where you will be. And I will see the blood, and I will pass over you. And the plague will not be with you to destroy, when I strike the land of Egypt. (Exo 12:13)
Hail Mary...

The Lord will cross through, striking the Egyptians. And when he will see the blood on the upper threshold, and on both the door posts, he will pass over the door of the house and not permit the Striker to enter into your houses or to do harm. (Exo 12:23)
Hail Mary...

Do not be afraid. Stand firm and see the great wonders of the Lord, which he will do today. For the enemy, whom you now see, will never again be seen, forever. The Lord will fight on your behalf, and you will remain silent. (Exo 14:13-14)
Hail Mary...

If you will listen to the voice of the Lord your God, and do what is right in his sight, and obey his commands, and keep all his precepts, I will not bring upon you any of the distress that I imposed on Egypt. For I am the Lord, your healer. (Exo 15:26)
Hail Mary...

How the Lord has given you the Sabbath, and, because of this, on the sixth day he distributes to you a double portion. Let each one remain with his own, and let no one go forth from his place on the seventh day. And the people rested on the seventh day. (Exo 16:29-30)
Hail Mary...

You have seen what I have done to the Egyptians, in what way I carried you upon the wings of eagles and how I have taken you for myself. (Exo 19:4)
Hail Mary...

Glory Be…

Decade 4
Our Father…

If, therefore, you will hear my voice, and you will keep my covenant, you will be to me a treasured possession out of all people. For all the earth is mine. And you will be to me a priestly kingdom and a holy nation. (Exo 19:5-6)
Hail Mary...

Go to the people, and sanctify them today, and tomorrow, and let them wash their garments. And let them be prepared on the third day. For on the third day, the Lord will descend, in the sight of all the people, over Mount Sinai. (Exo 19:10-11)
Hail Mary...

Honor your father and your mother, so that you may have a long life upon the land, which the Lord your God will give to you. (Exo 20:12)

Hail Mary...

For six days, you shall work. On the seventh day, you shall cease, so that your ox and your donkey may rest, and so that the newcomer and the child of your handmaid may be refreshed. (Exo 23:12)
Hail Mary...

Behold, I will send my Angel, who will go before you, and preserve you on your journey, and lead you into the place that I have prepared. (Exo 23:20)
Hail Mary...

If you listen to his voice and do all that I say, I will be an enemy to your enemies, and I will afflict those who afflict you. (Exo 23:22)
Hail Mary...

You shall worship the Lord your God, so that I may bless your bread and your waters, and so that I may take away sickness from your midst. There will not be fruitless or barren ones in your land. I will fill up the number of your days. (Exo 23:25-26)
Hail Mary...

You shall be holy unto me, because I, the Lord, am holy, and I have separated you from the other peoples, so that you would be mine. (Lev 20:26)
Hail Mary...

If you will walk in my precepts, and observe my commandments, and accomplish them, I will give to you rain in its time, and the ground shall bring forth its seedlings, and the trees shall be filled again with fruit. The threshing of the harvest shall last until the vintage, and the vintage shall overtake the sowing. And you shall eat your bread to fullness, and you shall live in your land without fear. (Lev 26:3-5)
Hail Mary...

I will set my tabernacle in your midst, and my soul will not cast you out. I will walk among you, and I will be your God, and you shall be my people. (Lev 26:11-12)
Hail Mary...

Glory Be…

Decade 5

Our Father…

I am the Lord your God, who led you away from the land of the Egyptians, to be their slaves no more, and I have broken the chains around your necks, so that you would walk upright. (Lev 26:13)
Hail Mary...

May the Lord bless you and keep you. May the Lord make his face to shine on you and be gracious to you. May the Lord lift up his countenance toward you and grant peace to you. (Num 6:24-26)
Hail Mary...

If you go forth to war from your land, against the enemies who set out against you, you shall sound the trumpets repeatedly, and there shall be a remembrance of you before the Lord your God, so that you may be rescued from the hands of your enemies. (Num 10:9)
Hail Mary...

Rise up, O Lord, and let your enemies be scattered, and let those who hate you flee from your face. (Num 10:35)
Hail Mary...

God is not like a man, so that he would lie, nor is he like a son of man, so that he would be changed. Therefore, having spoken, will he not act? Has he ever spoken, and not fulfilled? (Num 23:19)
Hail Mary...

May the Lord, the God of your fathers, add to this number many thousands more, and may he bless you, just as he has said. (Deut 1:11)
Hail Mary...

Have no dread or fear of them. The Lord God himself, who is your leader, will fight on your behalf, just as he did in Egypt in the sight of all. (Deut 1:29-30)
Hail Mary...

The Lord your God has blessed you in every work of your hands. The Lord your God, dwelling with you, knows your journey, how you crossed through this great wilderness over forty years, and how you have been lacking in nothing. (Deut 2:7)
Hail Mary...

You should not fear them. For the Lord your God will fight on your behalf. (Deut 3:22)
Hail Mary...

Listen to the precepts and ordinances which I am teaching to you, so that, by doing these, you may live, and you may enter and possess the land, which the Lord, the God of your ancestors, will give to you. (Deut 4:1)
Hail Mary...

Glory Be...

Day 2

Decade 1

Our Father…

For what great nation is there that has God so near as our God is, whenever we call to him. What other nation is there so renowned as to have laws, and statutes and the entire law that I will set forth today before your eyes? (Deut 4:7-8)

Hail Mary...

Guard yourself and your soul carefully. You should not forget the words that your eyes have seen, and do not let them be cut away from your heart, throughout all the days of your life. You shall teach them to your children and to your grandchildren. (Deut 4:9)

Hail Mary...

When you will seek the Lord your God in that place, you shall find him, if only you seek him with all your heart, and in all the tribulation of your soul. (Deut 4:29)

Hail Mary...

The Lord your God is a merciful God. He will not abandon you, nor will he entirely destroy you, nor will he forget the covenant, which he swore to your ancestors. (Deut 4:31)

Hail Mary...

Keep his precepts and commandments, which I am teaching to you, so that it may be well with you, and with your children after you, and so that you may remain for a long time upon the land, which the Lord your God will give to you. (Deut 4:40)

Hail Mary...

Who will grant to them to have such a mind, so that they may fear me, and may obey all my commandments at all times, so that it may be well with them and with their sons forever? (Deut 5:29)

Hail Mary...

Keep and do the things which the Lord God has commanded you. You shall not turn aside, neither to the right, nor to the left. For you shall walk in the way that the Lord your God has instructed, so that you may live, and it may be well with you, and that you may live long in the land that you are to possess. (Deut 5:32-33)

Hail Mary...

Keep these words, which I instruct to you this day, in your heart. And you shall explain them to your children. And you shall meditate upon them sitting in your house, and walking on a journey, when lying down and when rising up. And you shall bind them like a sign on your hand, and they shall be fixed as an emblem on your foreheads. And you shall write them at the threshold and on the doors of your house. (Deut 6:6-9)
Hail Mary...

You are a holy people to the Lord your God. The Lord your God has chosen you so that you would be his particular people out of all the peoples who are upon the earth. (Deut 7:6)
Hail Mary...

It is because the Lord has loved you, and has kept his oath, which he swore to your fathers, that he has led you away with a mighty hand, and he has redeemed you from the house of slavery. (Deut 7:8)
Hail Mary...

Glory Be...

Decade 2
Our Father...

You shall know that the Lord your God himself is a strong and faithful God, preserving his covenant and his mercy for those who love him and those who keep his commandments for a thousand generations. (Deut 7:9)
Hail Mary...

If, after you have heard these ordinances, you keep and do them, the Lord your God will also keep his covenant with you and the mercy that he swore to your fathers. (Deut 7:12)
Hail Mary...

He will love you and multiply you. And he will bless the fruit of your womb, and the fruit of your land: your grain as well as your vintage, oil, and herds, and the flocks of your sheep, upon the land about which he swore to your fathers that he would give it to you. (Deut 7:13)
Hail Mary...

Blessed shall you be among all peoples. with neither sterility nor barrenness among you or your livestock. The Lord will take all sickness away from you. And the very dreadful diseases of Egypt, which you have known, he will not bring upon you, but upon your enemies. (Deut 7:14-15)
Hail Mary...

Remember the entire journey along which the Lord your God led you, for forty years through the desert, in order to humble you, and to test you to make known the things that were in your heart, whether or not you would keep his commandments. (Deut 8:2)
Hail Mary...

Your clothes have not worn out and your feet did not swell these forty years. Recognize in your heart that, just as a parent disciplines his child, so has the Lord your God disciplined you. So therefore keep the commandments of the Lord your God, and walk in his ways and fear him. (Deut 8:4-6)
Hail Mary...

The Lord your God will lead you into a good land: a land of brooks and waters and fountains, in which deep rivers burst forth from its plains and mountains, a land of crops, barley, and vineyards, in which fig and pomegranate and olive trees spring up, a land of oil and honey. In that place, without any need, you shall eat your bread and enjoy an abundance of all things. (Deut 8:7-9)
Hail Mary...

Be observant and cautious, lest at some time you may forget the Lord your God, and neglect his commandments, as well as the ordinances and statutes, which I instruct to you this day. (Deut 8:11)
Hail Mary...

Remember the Lord your God, for it is he who gives power to get wealth, so that he may fulfill his covenant, about which he swore to your ancestors. (Deut 8:18)
Hail Mary...

What does the Lord your God require of you? Only that you fear the Lord your God, and walk in his ways, and love him, and serve the Lord your God with your whole heart and with your whole soul, and that you keep the commandments of the Lord, and his decrees, which I am instructing to you this day, so that it may be well with you. (Deut 10:12-13)
Hail Mary...

Glory Be…

Decade 3
Our Father…

The Lord your God himself is the God of gods, and the Lord of lords, a God great and powerful and awesome, who favors no person and accepts no bribe. (Deut 10:17)
Hail Mary...

Your eyes have seen all the great works of the Lord, which he has accomplished, so that you would keep all his commandments, which I entrust to you this day, and so that you would be able to enter and possess the land, toward which you are advancing. Deut 11:7-8)
Hail Mary...

So then, if you obey my commandments, which I am instructing to you this day, so that you love the Lord your God, and serve him with your whole heart and your whole soul, he will give to your land the early rain and the late rain, so that you may gather your grain, and your wine, and your oil, and your hay from the fields in order to feed your cattle, and so that you yourselves may eat and be satisfied. (Deut 11:13-15)
Hail Mary...

For if you keep the commandments which I am entrusting to you, and if you do them, so that you love the Lord your God, and walk in all his ways, clinging to him, the Lord will drive out all these nations before your face, and you shall possess them, though they are greater and stronger than you. (Deut 11:22-23)
Hail Mary...

Behold, I am setting before you today a blessing and a curse. It will be a blessing, if you obey the commandments of the Lord your God, which I am instructing to you this day. It will be a curse, if you do not obey the commandments of the Lord your God. (Deut 11:26-28)
Hail Mary...

You are a holy people, for the Lord your God. And he chose you, so that you may be a people particularly his, out of all the nations on earth. (Deut 14:2)
Hail Mary...

When the Lord your God has blessed you, as he promised you, you shall lend money to many nations, and you yourselves shall borrow in return from no one. You shall rule over very many nations, and no one shall rule over you. (Deut 15:6)
Hail Mary...

Give liberally and without grieving when you give: because for on this account the Lord your God shall bless you in all your works, and in all that you put your hand into. (Deut 15:10)
Hail Mary...

If you go out to battle against your enemies, and you see horsemen and chariots, and that the multitude of your adversary's army is greater than your own, you shall not fear them. For the Lord your God, who led you away from the land of Egypt, is with you. (Deut 20:1)

Hail Mary...

Look with favor from your sanctuary and from your lofty habitation amid the heavens, and bless your people Israel and the land which you have given to us, just as you swore to our fathers, a land flowing with milk and honey. (Deut 26:15)
Hail Mary...

Glory Be...

Decade 4

Our Father...

Today, the Lord has chosen you, so that you may be his particular people, just as he has spoken to you, and so that you may keep all his precepts. (Deut 26:18)
Hail Mary...

If you will listen to the voice of the Lord your God, so as to keep and do all of his commandments, which I instruct to you this day, the Lord your God will cause you to be more exalted than all the nations which exist upon the earth. (Deut 28:1)
Hail Mary...

Blessed shall you be in the city, and blessed in the field. Blessed shall be the fruit of your womb, and the fruit of your land, and the fruit of your cattle, the droves of your herds, and the folds of your sheep. Blessed shall be your barns, and blessed your storehouses. Blessed shall you be when you come in and when you go out. (Deut 28:2-6)
Hail Mary...

The Lord will grant that your enemies, who rise up against you, will be defeated in your sight. They will come against you by one way, and they will flee from your face by seven ways. (Deut 28:7)
Hail Mary...

The Lord will send forth a blessing upon your cellars, and upon all the works of your hands. And he will bless you in the land that you shall receive. (Deut 28:8)
Hail Mary...

All the peoples of the earth shall see that the name of the Lord has been invoked over you, and they shall fear you. (Deut 28:10)
Hail Mary...

The Lord will cause you to be abundant in every good thing: in the fruit of your womb, and in the fruit of your cattle, and in the fruit of your land, which the Lord swore to your ancestors that he would give to you. (Deut 28:11)
Hail Mary...

The Lord will open his excellent treasury, the heavens, so that it may distribute rain in due time. And he will bless all the works of your hands. And you shall lend to many nations, but you yourself will borrow nothing from anyone.. (Deut 28:12)
Hail Mary...

The Lord will appoint you as the head, and not as the tail. And you shall be always above, and not beneath. But only if you will listen to the commandments of the Lord your God, which I entrust to you this day, and will keep and do them. (Deut 28:13)
Hail Mary...

Keep the words of this covenant, and fulfill them, so that you may succeed in all that you are doing. (Deut 29:9)
Hail Mary...

Glory Be...

Decade 5

Our Father...

He will take you up and lead you into the land which your ancestors had possessed, and you shall obtain it. And in blessing you, he will make you greater in number than your ancestors ever were. The Lord your God will circumcise your heart, and the heart of your offspring, so that you may love the Lord your God with your entire heart and with your entire soul, so that you may be able to live. (Deut 30:5-6)
Hail Mary...

The Lord your God will cause you to abound in all the works of your hands, in the fruit of your womb, and in the fruit of your cattle, in the fertility of your land, and with an abundance of all things. For the Lord will return, so that he may rejoice over you in all good things, just as he rejoiced in your ancestors: but only if you will listen to the voice of the Lord your God, and keep his precepts and statues, which have been written in this law, and only if you return to the Lord your God with all your heart and with all your soul. (Deut 30:9-10)
Hail Mary...

I call heaven and earth as witnesses this day, that I have set before you life and death, blessing and curse. Therefore, choose life, so that both you and your offspring may live. (Deut 30:19)

Hail Mary...

Do not be afraid, and do not dread or have fear of them. For the Lord your God himself goes with you, and he will neither fail you nor abandon you. (Deut 31:6)
Hail Mary...

The Lord will go before you. He will himself be with you. He will neither renounce nor abandon you. Do not be afraid, and do not dread. (Deut 31:8)
Hail Mary...

He sustained him in a desert land, in a place of horror and a vast wilderness. He led him around and cared for him, and he guarded him like the pupil of his eye. (Deut 32:10)
Hail Mary...

Blessed are you. Who is like you, the people who are saved by the Lord? He is the shield of your help and the sword of your glory. Your enemies will refuse to acknowledge you, and so you shall tread upon their necks. (Deut 33:29)
Hail Mary...

No one will be able to resist you during all the days of your life. Just as I was with Moses, so will I be with you. I will not leave you, nor will I forsake you. Be strengthened and be steadfast. (Josh 1:5-6)
Hail Mary...

The book of this law shall not depart from your mouth. Instead, you shall meditate upon it, day and night, so that you may observe and do all the things that are written in it. Then you shall direct your way and understand it. (Josh 1:8)
Hail Mary...

Be strong and courageous; be not afraid, neither be dismayed: for the Lord your God is with you wherever you go. (Josh 1:9)
Hail Mary...

Glory Be…

Day 3

Decade 1

Our Father…

Be sanctified. For tomorrow the Lord will accomplish miracles among you. (Josh 3:5)

Hail Mary...

The Lord God will take away, in your sight, nations that are great and strong, and no one will be able to withstand you. (Josh 23:9)

Hail Mary...

One of you shall pursue a thousand men of the enemies. For the Lord your God himself will fight on your behalf, just as he promised. (Josh 23:10)

Hail Mary...

Today I am entering the way of the entire earth, and you shall know with all your mind that, out of all the words that the Lord has promised to fulfill for you, not one will pass by unfulfilled. (Josh 23:14)

Hail Mary...

The Lord will judge the parts of the earth, and he will give dominion to his king, and he will lift up the power of his anointed. (1 Sam 2:10)

Hail Mary...

If you would return to the Lord with your whole heart, take away strange gods from among you, and prepare your hearts for the Lord, and serve him alone, he will rescue you from the hand of the enemies. (1 Sam 7:3)

Hail Mary...

Do not be afraid. You have done all this evil. Yet truly, do not turn aside from following the Lord. Instead, serve the Lord with all your heart. And do not choose to turn aside after vanities, which will never benefit you, nor rescue you, since they are useless. And the Lord will not abandon his people, because of his great name. For the Lord has sworn to make you his people. (1 Sam 12:20-22)

Hail Mary...

Does the Lord want burnt offerings and sacrifices, and not instead that the voice of the Lord should be obeyed? For obedience is better than sacrifice. And to heed is greater than to offer the fat of rams. (1 Sam 15:22)

Hail Mary...

Whenever the evil spirit from the Lord assailed Saul, David took up his stringed instrument, and he struck it with his hand, and Saul was refreshed and uplifted. For the evil spirit withdrew from him. (1 Sam 16:23)
Hail Mary...

May you be blessed by the Lord. For you have shown me compassion. (1 Sam 23:21)
Hail Mary...

Glory Be...

Decade 2

Our Father...

When your days will have been fulfilled, and you will sleep with your fathers, I will raise up your offspring after you, who will go forth from your loins, and I will make firm his kingdom. He himself shall build a house to my name. And I will establish the throne of his kingdom forever. (2 Sam 7:12-13)
Hail Mary...

Bless the house of your servant, so that it may be forever before you. For you, O Lord God, have spoken. And so, let the house of your servant be blessed with your blessing forever. (2 Sam 7:29)
Hail Mary...

I will call upon the Lord, who is worthy to be praised; and I will be saved from my enemies. (2 Sam 22:4)
Hail Mary...

The Lord will reward me according to my righteousness. And he will repay me according to the cleanness of my hands. For I have kept to the ways of the Lord, and I have not acted impiously before my God. (2 Sam 22:21)
Hail Mary...

Who is God except the Lord? And who is a rock, except our God? He has girded me with strength, and he has made my way perfect: making my feet like the feet of deer, and stationing me upon my exalted places, teaching my hands to do battle, and making my arms like a bow of brass. (2 Sam 22:32-35)
Hail Mary...

The Spirit of the Lord speaks through me, and his word is spoken through my tongue. (2 Sam 23:2)
Hail Mary...

In that place, David built an altar to the Lord. And he offered burnt offerings and peace offerings. And the Lord was gracious to the land, and the plague was held back from Israel. (2 Sam 24:25)
Hail Mary...

Observe the charge of the Lord your God, so that you walk in his ways, so that you keep his statutes, and his precepts, and ordinances, just as it is written in the law of Moses. So that you may prosper in everything that you do and wherever you turn. (1 Kgs 2:3)
Hail Mary...

If you will walk in my ways, and keep my precepts and my commandments, just as your father walked, I will lengthen your days. (1 kgs 3:14)
Hail Mary...

I will dwell in the midst of the children of Israel, and I will not forsake my people. (1 Kgs 6:13)
Hail Mary...

Glory Be...

Decade 3

Our Father...

Look with favor upon the prayer of your servant and upon his petitions, O Lord, my God. Listen to the cry and the prayer, which your servant prays before you this day, so that your eyes may be open over this house, night and day, over the house about which you said, 'My name shall be there,' so that you may heed the prayer that your servant is praying in this place to you. (1 Kgs 8:28-29)
Hail Mary...

Hear from heaven, and forgive the sins of your servants and of your people. And reveal to them the good way, along which they should walk, and grant rain upon your land, which you have given to your people as a possession. (1 Kgs 8:36)
Hail Mary...

May your eyes be open to the supplication of your servant and of your people. And so may you heed them in all the things about which they will call upon you. (1 Kgs 8:52)
Hail Mary...

Blessed is the Lord, who has given rest to his people Israel, in accord with all that he said. Not even one word, out of all the good things that he spoke by his servant Moses, has fallen away. (1 kgs 8:56)
Hail Mary...

May the Lord our God be with us, just as he was with our ancestors, not abandoning us, and not rejecting us. But may he incline our hearts to himself, so that we may walk in all his ways, and keep his commandments, and his decrees, and whatever ordinances he commanded to our fathers. (1 Kgs 8:57-58)
Hail Mary...

May these my words, by which I have prayed before the Lord, be near to the Lord our God, day and night, so that he may maintain the cause of his servant and of his people, throughout each day. (1 Kgs 8:59)
Hail Mary...

The jar of flour will not fail, nor the bottle of oil be diminished, until the day when the Lord will grant rain upon the face of the earth. (1 Kgs 17:14)
Hail Mary...

While the musician was playing, the power of the Lord fell upon him. (2 Kgs 3:15)
Hail Mary...

He clung to the Lord, and he did not withdraw from his footsteps, and he carried out his commandments, which the Lord had instructed to Moses. Therefore, the Lord was also with him. wherever he went, he prospered (2 Kgs 18:6-7)
Hail Mary...

Your heart was terrified, and you humbled yourself before the Lord, listening to the words against this place and its inhabitants, specifically, that they would become an astonishment and a curse, and because you have torn your garments, and have wept before me: I also have heard you, says the Lord. (2 Kgs 22:19)
Hail Mary...

Glory Be…

Decade 4

Our Father…

If only, when blessing, you will bless me, and will broaden my borders, and your hand will be with me, and you will keep me from hurt and harm. (1 Chron 4:10)
Hail Mary...

The ark of God dwelt in the house of Obededom for three months. And the Lord blessed his house and all that he had. (1 Chron 13:14)
Hail Mary...

I have given a place to my people Israel. They shall be planted, and they shall live in it, and they shall no longer be moved. (1 Chron 17:9)
Hail Mary...

Let it please you to bless the house of your servant, so that it may be always before you. For since it is you who is blessing, O Lord, it shall be blessed forever. (1 Chron 17:27)
Hail Mary...

May the Lord give you prudence and understanding, so that you may be able to rule and to guard the law of the Lord your God. For then you will be able to prosper, if you keep the commandments and judgments that the Lord instructed. Be strong and of good courage. You should not fear, and you should not dread. (1 Chron 22:12-13)
Hail Mary...

Know the God of your father and serve him with a perfect heart and a willing mind. For the Lord searches every mind and understands every thought and plan. If you seek him, you will find him. But if you abandon him, he will cast you aside for eternity.(1 Chron 28:9)
Hail Mary...

Be strong and of good courage, and act. You should not be afraid, and you should not be dismayed. For the Lord my God will be with you, and he will not send you away, nor will he abandon you, until you have finished the entire work for the service of the house of the Lord. (1 Chron 28:20)
Hail Mary...

Blessed are you, O Lord God of Israel, our Father from eternity to eternity. Yours, O Lord, is the greatness, the power, the glory, the victory, and to you is praise. For all the things that are in heaven and on earth are yours. Yours is the kingdom, O Lord, and you are above all rulers. (1 Chron 29:10-11)
Hail Mary...

Riches and honor come from you. You have dominion over all things. In your hand is virtue and power. In your hand is greatness and authority over all things. Now therefore, we give thanks to you, our God, and we praise your glorious name. (1 Chron 29:12-13)
Hail Mary...

When they all sounded out together, with trumpets, and voice, and cymbals, and pipes, and with various kinds of musical instruments, lifting their voice on high, the sound was heard from far away, so that when they had begun to praise the Lord, and to say, "praise to the Lord, for he is good; for his steadfast love is eternal," the house of God was filled with a cloud. (2 Chron 5:13)

Hail Mary...

Glory Be...

Decade 5

Our Father...

If they will repent, with their whole heart and with their whole soul, in the land of their captivity to which they were led away, and if they will pray toward their own land, which you gave to their ancestors, and of the city, which you have chosen, and of the house, which I have built to your name, then you will heed their prayers from heaven, that is, from your dwelling place, and you will maintain their cause and you will forgive your people, even though they have sinned against you. (2 Chron 6:38-39)
Hail Mary...

If my people, over whom my name has been invoked, being converted, will have petitioned me and sought my face, and will have done penance for their wicked ways, then I will heed them from heaven, and I will forgive their sins, and I will heal their land. (2 Chron 7:14)
Hail Mary...

When the Lord had seen that they were humbled, the word of the Lord came saying: "Because they have been humbled, I will not disperse them. And I will give to them a little help, and my fury will not rain down upon Jerusalem." (2 Chron 12:7)
Hail Mary...

Yet truly, because they were humbled, the wrath of the Lord turned away from them, and so they were not utterly destroyed. (2 Chron 12:12)
Hail Mary...

The eyes of the Lord contemplate the entire earth, and offer strength to those who believe in him with a perfect heart. (2 Chron 16:9)
Hail Mary...

Do not be afraid. Neither should you be dismayed by this multitude. For the fight is not yours, but God's. (2 Chron 20:15)
Hail Mary...

He appointed the singing men of the Lord, so that they would praise him by their companies, and so that they would go before the army. And when they had begun to sing praises, the Lord turned their ambushes upon themselves, and they were struck down. (2 Chron 20:21-22)
Hail Mary...

The Lord your God is compassionate and merciful, and he will not turn away his face from you, if you will return to him. (2 Chron 30:9)
Hail Mary...

Your heart was penitent, and you humbled yourself in the sight of God, and since, revering my face, you have torn your garments, and have wept before me: I also have heeded you, says the Lord. (2 Chron 34:27)
Hail Mary...

If you will return to me, and keep my precepts, and do them, even if you will have been led away to the furthest reaches of the heavens, I will gather you from there, and I will lead you back to the place that I have chosen so that my name would dwell there. (Neh 1:9)
Hail Mary...

Glory Be...

Day 4

Decade 1

Our Father…

The joy of the Lord is our strength. (Neh 8:10)
Hail Mary...

You gave them your good Spirit, so that he might teach them. (Neh 9:20)
Hail Mary...

If we obey God, and withdraw from all sin, and do what is good, he will be pleased with us and make us prosperous. (Tob 4:21)
Hail Mary...

Your power, O Lord, is not in numbers, nor is your will with the powerful, nor from the beginning have the arrogant been pleasing to you. But the pleas of the humble and the meek have always pleased you. O God of the heavens, Creator of the waters, and Lord of all creation, hear my prayer. (Judith 9:11-12)
Hail Mary...

Then they all together praised the merciful Lord, and were strengthened in their souls, being prepared to break through not only men, but also the most ferocious beasts and walls of iron. (2 Mac 11:9)
Hail Mary...

As for me, I will beg the Lord, and state my plea before God. He does great and unfathomable and miraculous things without number. (Job 5:8-9)
Hail Mary...

He places the humble on high and and those who mourn are lifted to safety. (Job 5:11)
Hail Mary...

Your hands have made me and formed me all around, and, in this way, do you suddenly throw me away? Remember that you have fashioned me like clay; and will you reduce me to dust? Have you not extracted me like milk and curdled me like cheese? You have clothed me with skin and flesh. You have put me together with bones and nerves. You have assigned to me life and mercy, and your visitation has preserved my spirit. (Job 10:8-12)
Hail Mary...

I know that my Redeemer lives, And He shall stand at last on the earth. (Job 19:25)
Hail Mary...

The Lord restored the fortunes of Job, when he prayed for his friends. And the Lord gave to Job twice as much as he had before. (Job 42:10)
Hail Mary...

Glory Be…

Decade 2

Our Father…

Blessed is the man who has not followed the counsel of the wicked, and has not remained in the way of sinners, and has not sat in the chair of scoffers. But his will is with the law of the Lord, and he will meditate on his law, day and night. (Ps 1:1-2)
Hail Mary...

His will is with the law of the Lord, and he will meditate on his law, day and night. And he will be like a tree that has been planted beside running waters, which will provide its fruit in its time, and its leaf will not fall away, and all things whatsoever that he does will prosper. (Ps 1:2-3)
Hail Mary...

You, Lord, are my supporter, my glory, and the one who raises up my head. (Ps 3:3)
Hail Mary...

I laid down and slept; I woke again; for the Lord sustained me. (Ps 3:5)
Hail Mary...

I will sleep and I will rest in peace. For you, O Lord, make me lie down in safety. (Ps 4:8)
Hail Mary...

Let all those who hope in you rejoice. They will exult in eternity, and you will dwell in them. And all those who love your name will glory in you. (Ps 5:11)
Hail Mary...

You will bless the righteous, O Lord. You surround them with favor as with a shield. (Ps 5:12)
Hail Mary...

What is man, that you are mindful of him, or the son of man, that you care for him? You reduced him to a little less than the Angels; you have crowned

him with glory and honor, and you have set him over the works of your hands. (Ps 8:4-5)
Hail Mary...

The Lord is a refuge for the oppressed, a stronghold in times of tribulation. (Ps 9:9)
Hail Mary...

Those who know your name put their hope in you. For you have not abandoned those seeking you, Lord. (Ps 9:10-11)
Hail Mary...

Glory Be…

Decade 3

Our Father…

Have mercy upon me, O Lord; see my trouble which I suffer of them that hate me You have lifted me up from the gates of death, so that I may announce all your praises. (Ps 9:13)
Hail Mary...

You do see, for you examine hardship and sorrow, so that you may take it into your hands. The poor one commits himself to you. You will be a helper to the orphan. (Ps 10:14)
Hail Mary...

The Lord will hear the desire of the poor. He will strengthen their heart, he will listen so as to judge for the orphan and the oppressed. (Ps 10:17)
Hail Mary...

The promises of the Lord are pure promises, silver tested by fire, purged from the earth, refined seven times. (Ps 12:6)
Hail Mary...

I will sing to the Lord, who assigns good things to me. And I will sing psalms to the name of the Lord Most High. (Ps 13:6)
Hail Mary...

O Lord, who will dwell in your tabernacle? Or who will rest on your holy mountain? He who walks without blemish and who works justice. He who speaks the truth in his heart, who has not acted deceitfully with his tongue, and has not done evil to his neighbor, and has not taken up a reproach against his neighbors. (Ps 15:1-3)
Hail Mary...

I will bless the Lord, who has bestowed understanding upon me. Moreover, my heart has also instructed me, even through the night. (Ps 16:7)
Hail Mary...

I keep the Lord always in my sight. For he is at my right hand, so that I may not be moved. Because of this, my heart has been joyful, and my soul rejoices. Moreover, even my body will rest in hope. (Ps 16:8-9)
Hail Mary...

You have made known to me the ways of life; there is fullness of joy in your presence. At your right hand are delights, even to the end. (Ps 16:11)
Hail Mary...

I will call upon the Lord, who is worthy to be praised: so shall I be saved from my enemies. (Ps 18:3)
Hail Mary...

Glory Be…

Decade 4

Our Father…

He delivered me, because he delighted in me. (Ps 18:19)
Hail Mary...

You will deliver the humble people, but you will bring down the eyes of the arrogant. (Ps 18:27)
Hail Mary...

As for my God, his way is undefiled. The promises of the Lord have been proved true. He is the protector of all who hope in him. (Ps 18:30)
Hail Mary...

Who is God, except the Lord? And who is God, except our God? It is God who has wrapped me with strength and made my way safe. It is he who has secured my feet, like the feet of deer, and who set me secure upon the heights. It is he who trains my hands for battle. So that my arms can bend a bow of bronze. (Ps 18:31-34)
Hail Mary...

You have wrapped me with strength for the battle. And those rising up against me, you have subdued under me. (Ps 18:39)
Hail Mary...

The law of the Lord is perfect, reviving souls. The testimony of the Lord is faithful, providing wisdom to little ones; the justice of the Lord are right,

rejoicing hearts; the precepts of the Lord is clear, enlightening the eyes. (Ps 19:7-8)
Hail Mary...

The fear of the Lord is pure, enduring for all generations. The judgments of the Lord are true and righteous altogether. Desirable beyond gold and many precious stones, and sweeter than honey and the honeycomb. (Ps 19:9-10)
Hail Mary...

May he grant to you according to your heart's desires, and fulfill all your plans. We will rejoice in your salvation, and in the name of our God, we will be magnified. May the Lord fulfill all your petitions. (Ps 20:4-5)
Hail Mary...

For you will give him as a blessing forever and ever. You will make him rejoice with gladness in your presence. (Ps 21:6)
Hail Mary...

In you, our ancestors have trusted. They trusted, and you freed them. They cried out to you, and they were saved. In you, they trusted and were not put to shame. (Ps 22:4-5)
Hail Mary...

Glory Be...

Decade 5

Our Father...

The poor will eat and be satisfied, and those who yearn for the Lord will praise him. Their hearts will live forever and ever. (Ps 22:26)
Hail Mary...

All the ends of the earth will remember, and they will turn to the Lord. And all the families of the nations shall worship before him. (Ps 22:27)
Hail Mary...

The Lord is my shepherd; I shall not want. He makes me to lie down in green pastures: he leads me beside the still waters. He restores my soul: he leads me in the paths of righteousness for his name's sake. (Ps 23:1-3)
Hail Mary...

Even though I walk through the valley of the shadow of death, I will fear no evil: for you are with me; Your rod and your staff they comfort me. (Ps 23:4)
Hail Mary...

You prepare a table before me in the presence of my enemies: You anoint my head with oil; my cup runs over. Surely goodness and mercy shall follow

me all the days of my life: and I will dwell in the house of the Lord forever. (Ps 23:5-6)
Hail Mary...

The innocent of hands and the pure of heart, who has not lifted up his soul to falsehood, nor sworn deceitfully. He will receive a blessing from the Lord and mercy from God, his Savior. (Ps 24:4-5)
Hail Mary...

He will direct the humble in what is right. He will teach the meek his ways. (Ps 25:9)
Hail Mary...

Which is the man who fears the Lord? He will teach them the way that they should choose. His soul will dwell upon good things, and his offspring will inherit the earth. (Ps 25:12-13)
Hail Mary...

My eyes are ever toward the Lord, for he will pull my feet from the snare. (Ps 25:15)
Hail Mary...

The Lord is my light and my salvation, whom shall I fear? The Lord is the strength of my life, of whom shall I be afraid? (Ps 27:1)
Hail Mary...

Glory Be...

Day 5

Decade 1

Our Father…

Though an army should encamp against me, my heart shall not fear: though war should rise against me, yet I will be confident. (Ps 27:3)
Hail Mary...

In the time of trouble He will hide me in His shelter; In the secret place of His tabernacle He will hide me; He will set me high upon a rock. (Ps 27:5)
Hail Mary...

If my father and mother forsake me, then the Lord will take me up. (Ps 27:10)
Hail Mary...

I believe that I shall see the good things of the Lord in the land of the living. Wait for the Lord, be strong; and let your heart take courage, and wait for the Lord. (Ps 27:13-14)
Hail Mary...

The Lord is my helper and my protector. In him, my heart has hoped and I have been helped. And my flesh has flourished again, and with my song I give thanks to him. (Ps 28:7)
Hail Mary...

The Lord sits upon the flood. And the Lord will sit as King in eternity. The Lord will give strength to his people. The Lord will bless his people in peace. (Ps 29:10-11)
Hail Mary...

O Lord my God, I cried to you for help, and you have healed me. O Lord, you brought up my soul from Sheol, restored me to life from among those gone down to the Pit. (Ps 30:1-2)
Hail Mary...

Sing praises to the Lord, you his saints, and give thanks with remembrance of his holiness. For wrath is in his indignation, and his favor is for a lifetime. Toward evening, weeping will linger, and toward morning, gladness. (Ps 30:4-5)
Hail Mary...

You have turned my mourning into gladness. You have taken off my sackcloth, and you have surrounded me with joy. So then, may my soul

praise you and not be quiet. O Lord, my God, I will give thanks to you for eternity. (Ps 30:11-12)
Hail Mary...

You are my strength and my refuge; and for the sake of your name, you will lead me and nourish me. You will lead me out of this snare, which they have hidden for me. For you are my protector. (Ps 31:3-4)
Hail Mary...

Glory Be...

Decade 2

Our Father...

I will exult and rejoice in your steadfast love. For you have looked upon my affliction; you have saved my soul from adversities. And you have not delivered me in the hands of the enemy. You have set my feet in a broad place. (Ps 31:7-8)
Hail Mary...

Into your hands, I commend my spirit. You have redeemed me, O Lord, faithful God. (Ps 31:5)
Hail Mary...

Let your face shine on your servant; save me in your unfailing love. (Ps 31:16)
Hail Mary...

How great is the multitude of your goodness, O Lord, which you have laid for those who fear you, which you have perfected for those who hope in you, in the sight of everyone. (Ps 31:19)
Hail Mary...

You hide them in the shelter of your presence, from the plots of human. You protect them in your shelter, from contentious tongues. (Ps 31:20)
Hail Mary...

Let your heart be strengthened, all you who hope in the Lord. (Ps 31:24)
Hail Mary...

Blessed are they whose transgressions have been forgiven and whose sins have been covered. Blessed is the man to whom the Lord imputes no sin, and in whose spirit there is no deceit. (Ps 32:1-2)
Hail Mary...

I said, "I will confess my transgressions to the Lord," and you forgave the guilt of my sin. (Ps 32:5)
Hail Mary...

You are my hiding place; You preserve me from trouble; You encompass me with songs of deliverance. (Ps 32:7)
Hail Mary...

I will instruct you and teach you in the way which you should go: I will guide you with my eyes upon you. (Ps 32:8)
Hail Mary...

Glory Be...

Decade 3

Our Father...

Many torments shall be to the wicked: but steadfast love shall surround him who trusts in the Lord. (Ps 32:10)
Hail Mary...

The word of the Lord is upright, and all his works are in faith. (Ps 33:4)
Hail Mary...

Fear the Lord, all you his holy ones. For there is no destitution for those who fear him. The rich have been needy and hungry, but those who seek the Lord will not be deprived of any good thing. (Ps 33:9-10)
Hail Mary...

Blessed is the nation whose God is the Lord, the people whom he has chosen as his inheritance. (Ps 33:12)
Hail Mary...

Behold, the eye of the Lord is upon them that fear him, upon them that hope in his steadfast love; To deliver their soul from death, and to keep them alive in famine. (Ps 33:18-19)
Hail Mary...

I sought the Lord, and he answered me, and he delivered me from all my fears. (Ps 34:4)
Hail Mary...

This poor man cried out, and the Lord heard him, and he saved him out of all his troubles. (Ps 34:6)
Hail Mary...

The Angel of the Lord will encamp around those who fear him, and he will deliver them. (Ps 34:7)
Hail Mary...

O fear the Lord, all you saints: for those who fear him have no want. (Ps 34:9)
Hail Mary...

The young lion lacks and suffers hunger: but those who seek the Lord shall not lack any good thing. (Ps 34:10)
Hail Mary...

Glory Be...

Decade 4

Our Father...

The eyes of the Lord are on the just, and his ears are open their cries. (Ps 34:15)
Hail Mary...

The just cried out, and the Lord heard them, and he freed them from all their troubles. (Ps 34:17)
Hail Mary...

The Lord is near to those who are troubled in heart, and he will save the crushed in spirit. (Ps 34:18)
Hail Mary...

Many are the afflictions of the just, but from them all the Lord will free them. The Lord preserves all of their bones, not one of them shall be broken. (Ps 34:19)
Hail Mary...

The Lord will redeem the soul of his servants, and none of those who hope in him will be condemned. (Ps 34:22)
Hail Mary...

Trust in the Lord and do good, so you will live in the land, and so you shall enjoy security. (Ps 37:3)
Hail Mary...

Delight in the Lord, and he will give you the desires of your heart. (Ps 37:4)
Hail Mary...

Commit your way to the Lord, and hope in him, and he will accomplish it. And he will bring forth your justice like the light, and your judgment like the noonday. (Ps 37:5-6)
Hail Mary...

The Lord knows the days of the blameless, and their inheritance will be in eternity. They will not be confounded in an evil time; and in days of famine, they will be satisfied. (Ps 37:18-19)
Hail Mary...

The steps of a man will be directed by the Lord, when he delights in his way. When he falls, he will not be utterly cast down, because the Lord upholds him with his hand. (Ps 37:23-24)
Hail Mary...

Glory Be…

Decade 5
Our Father…

I have been young, and now I am old; and I have not seen the righteous forsaken, nor their children begging bread. They show compassion and lend, all day long, and their children will be in blessing. (Ps 37:25-26)
Hail Mary...

For the Lord loves justice, and he will not abandon his faithful ones. They will be kept safe in eternity. (Ps 37:28)
Hail Mary...

The mouth of the righteous speaks wisdom, and his tongue talks of justice. The law of his God is in his heart; none of his steps shall slip. (Ps 37:30-31)
Hail Mary...

Wait for the Lord, and keep to his way. And he will exalt you to inherit the land. (Ps 37:34)
Hail Mary...

I have waited expectantly for the Lord, and he was attentive to me. And he heard my prayers and he led me out of the pit of misery and the miry bog. And he stationed my feet upon a rock, and he directed my steps. (Ps 40:1-2)
Hail Mary...

He sent a new song into my mouth, a song of praise to our God. Many will see, and they will fear; and they will hope in the Lord. (Ps 40:3)
Hail Mary...

Do you not know, or have you not heard? The Lord is the eternal God, who has created the limits of the earth. He does not diminish, and he does not struggle. Neither is his wisdom searchable. (Ps 40:28)
Hail Mary...

Blessed is he who shows understanding toward the needy and the poor. The Lord will deliver him in the evil day. May the Lord preserve him and give him life, and make him blessed upon the earth. And may he not hand him over to the will of his adversaries. (Ps 41:1-2)
Hail Mary...

The Lord will sustain them upon their sickbed. In their illness you heal all their infirmities. (Ps 41:3)
Hail Mary...

Why are you sad, my soul? And why do you disquiet me? Hope in God, for I will still give praise to him: the salvation of my countenance and my God. (Ps 43:5)
Hail Mary...

Glory Be...

Day 6

Decade 1

Our Father…

With you, we will push down our enemies; and in your name, we tread down those rising up against us. (Ps 44:5)
Hail Mary...

Our God is our refuge and strength, a helper in the tribulations that have greatly overwhelmed us. Because of this, we will not be afraid when the earth will be turbulent and the mountains will be transferred into the heart of the sea. (Ps 46:1-2)
Hail Mary...

Those who offer thanksgiving as a sacrifice honor me. Those who go the right way, I will reveal to him the salvation of God. (Ps 50:23)
Hail Mary...

Have mercy on me, O God, according to your steadfast love. And, according to the multitude of your compassion, blot out my transgressions. (Ps 51:1)
Hail Mary...

Sprinkle me with hyssop, and I will be cleansed. Wash me, and I will be made whiter than snow. Let me hear gladness and joy. And the bones that have been crushed will rejoice. (Ps 51:7-8)
Hail Mary...

Create a clean heart in me, O God. And renew an upright spirit within my inmost being. Do not cast me away from your presence; and do not take your Holy Spirit from me. Restore to me the joy of your salvation, and sustain me with a willing spirit. (Ps 51:10-12)
Hail Mary...

Cast your burden on the Lord, and he will sustain you. He will not permit the righteous to be moved. (Ps 55:22)
Hail Mary...

In God, whose Word I praise. In God, I have put my trust. I will not fear what flesh can do to me. (Ps 56:4)
Hail Mary...

You have kept count of my wanderings; put my tears into your bottle. Are they not in your book? (Ps 56:8)

Hail Mary...

In God, I have trusted. I will not fear what man can do to me. (Ps 56:11)
Hail Mary...

Glory Be...

Decade 2

Our Father...

Be merciful to me, O God, be merciful to me. For my soul trusts in you. And I will hope in the shadow of your wings, until the storms passes away. (Ps 57:1)
Hail Mary...

My soul waits in silence for God alone. For from him is my salvation. Yes, he alone is my rock and my salvation. He is my fortress; I will never be moved. Yet, truly, My soul waits for God alone. For from him is my hope. For he is my rock and my Savior. He is my fortress; I will not be moved. In God is my salvation and my glory. He is the God of my help, and my hope is in God. (Ps 62:1-2,5-7)
Hail Mary...

If I have cherished iniquity in my heart, the Lord would not listened. And yet, God has heeded me and he has attended to the voice of my supplication. (Ps 66:18-19)
Hail Mary...

May God rise up, and may his enemies be scattered, and may those who hate him flee from before his face. Just as smoke vanishes, so may they vanish. Just as wax flows away before the face of fire, so may the wicked perish before the face of God. (Ps 68:1-2)
Hail Mary...

God gives the solitary a home to live in. he brings out those who are bound with chains to prosperity. (Ps 68:6)
Hail Mary...

O God, you showered rain in plenty, whereby you restored your inheritance when it languished. Your people found a dwelling in it: In your goodness, O God, you have provided for the needy. (Ps 68:9-10)
Hail Mary...

As for me, my prayer is to you, O Lord. At an acceptable time, O God, in the abundance of your steadfast love, answer me. (Ps 69:13)
Hail Mary...

I will praise the name of God with a song, and I will magnify him with praise. Let the oppressed see and rejoice. You who seek God, let your hearts revive (Ps 69:30,32)
Hail Mary...

For you, O Lord, are my hope: my trust from my youth, O Lord. In you, I have been confirmed from my birth. You took me out of my mother's womb, you are my protector. In you, I will praise forever. (Ps 71:5-8)
Hail Mary...

He will free the poor from the powerful, and the poor one who has no helper. He will spare the poor and the indigent, and he will bring salvation to the souls of the poor. He will redeem their souls from oppression and from iniquity, and their names shall be honorable in his sight. (Ps 72:12-14)
Hail Mary...

Glory Be...

Decade 3

Our Father...

How good is God to Israel, to those who are upright in heart, to those who are pure in heart. (Ps 73:1)
Hail Mary...

My flesh and my heart may fail: but God is the strength of my heart, and my portion for ever. (Ps 73:26)
Hail Mary...

I cried out to the Lord with my voice, to God with my voice, and he attended to me. (Ps 77:1)
Hail Mary...

He rained down manna upon them to eat, and he gave them the bread of heaven. Man ate the bread of Angels. He sent them provisions in abundance. (Ps 78:24-25)
Hail Mary...

He is merciful, and he will pardon our sins. And he will not destroy us. And he has abundantly turned aside his own anger. And he did not enflame his wrath entirely. (Ps 78:38)
Hail Mary...

Do not remember against us the iniquities of our ancestors. May your mercies quickly meet us, for we have become exceedingly poor. (Ps 79:8)
Hail Mary...

Help us, O God, our Savior. And free us, Lord, for the glory of your name. And forgive us our sins for the sake of your name. (Ps 79:9)
Hail Mary...

How beloved is your dwelling place, O Lord of hosts! My soul longs and faints for the courts of the Lord. My heart and my flesh have exulted in the living God. (Ps 84:1-2)
Hail Mary...

One day in your courts is better than thousands elsewhere. I have chosen to be lowly in the house of my God, rather than to dwell in the tabernacles of sinners. (Ps 84:10)
Hail Mary...

The Lord God is a sun and shield; He will not withhold good things from those who walk uprightly. O Lord of hosts, blessed is the man who hopes in you. (Ps 84:11-12)
Hail Mary...

Glory Be…

Decade 4

Our Father…

You are good and forgiving, Lord, and plentiful in steadfast love to all who call upon you. (Ps 86:5)
Hail Mary...

I will give thanks to you, O Lord my God, with my whole heart. And I will glorify your name in eternity. For your steadfast love toward me is great, and you have rescued my soul. (Ps 86:12-13)
Hail Mary...

Satisfy us in the morning with your steadfast love; that we may rejoice and be glad all our days. (Ps 90:14)
Hail Mary...

He who dwells in the secret place of the most High shall abide under the shadow of the Almighty, will say of the Lord, He is my refuge and my fortress: my God; in him will I trust. (Ps 91:1-2)
Hail Mary...

You will not fear before the terror of the night, before the arrow flying in the day, before the pestilence that stalks in the darkness, nor the destruction of the noonday. (Ps 91:5-6)
Hail Mary...

A thousand will fall before your side and ten thousand at your right hand. Yet it will not draw near you. So then, truly, you will look with your eyes, and you will see the punishment of the wicked. (Ps 91:7-8)
Hail Mary...

For you, O Lord, are my refuge. You have set the Most High as your dwelling place, no evil will draw near to you, and the scourge will not approach your tent. (Ps 91:9-10)
Hail Mary...

He shall give his angels charge over you, to keep you in all your ways. They shall bear you up in their hands, lest you dash your foot against a stone. (Ps 91:11-12)
Hail Mary...

Those who love me, I will deliver. I will protect him because he has known my name. He will cry out to me, and I will answer him. I am with him in trouble. I will rescue him, and I will honor him. I will fill him with length of days. And I will reveal to him my salvation. (Ps 91:14-16)
Hail Mary...

The just one will flourish like the palm tree. He will be multiplied like the cedar of Lebanon. Those planted in the house of the Lord will flourish in the courts of the house of our God. They will still bear fruit in old age, and they will endure well. (Ps 92:12-14)
Hail Mary...

Glory Be...

Decade 5
Our Father...

The Lord will not cast off his people; he will not forsake his heritage; for justice shall return to the righteous, and all the upright in heart shall follow it. (Ps 94:14-15)
Hail Mary...

If ever I said, "My foot is slipping," then your steadfast love, O Lord, assisted me. (Ps 94:18)
Hail Mary...

According to the multitude of my sorrows in my heart, your consolations have given joy to my soul. (Ps 94:19)
Hail Mary...

The Lord watches over the souls of his holy ones. He will free them from the hand of the sinner. (Ps 97:10)

Hail Mary...

Worship the Lord joyfully, all the earth. Serve the Lord with rejoicing. Enter into his presence with singing. (Ps 100:2)
Hail Mary...

Enter his gates with thanksgiving, his courts with praise, and acknowledge him. Bless his name. (Ps 100:4)
Hail Mary...

My eyes looked toward the faithful of the earth, to live with me. The one who walks blamelessly will minister to me. (Ps 101:6)
Hail Mary...

He has noticed the prayer of the destitute, and he has not despised their petition. (Ps 102:17)
Hail Mary...

He has gazed from his high sanctuary. From heaven, the Lord has beheld the earth. So may he hear the groans of those in shackles, in order that he may release those who were doomed to die. (Ps 102:19-20)
Hail Mary...

Bless the Lord, O my soul, and do not forget all his benefits. He forgives all your iniquities. He heals all your infirmities. (Ps 103:2-3)
Hail Mary...

Glory Be...

Day 7

Decade 1

Our Father…

He heals all your infirmities. He redeems your life from destruction. He crowns you with mercy and compassion. He satisfies your desire with good things. (Ps 103:4-5)
Hail Mary...

He has not dealt with us according to our sins, and he has not repaid us according to our iniquities. (Ps 103:10)
Hail Mary...

As far as the east is from the west, so far has he removed our iniquities from us. (Ps 103:12)
Hail Mary...

As a father is compassionate to his children, so has the Lord been compassionate to those who fear him. For he knows our form. He has called to mind that we are dust. (Ps 103:13-14)
Hail Mary...

The mercy of the Lord is from eternity, and even unto eternity, upon those who fear him. And his justice is with the children's children, with those who serve his covenant and have been mindful of his commandments by doing them. (Ps 103:17-18)
Hail Mary...

You will send forth your Spirit, and they will be created. And you will renew the face of the earth. (Ps 104:30)
Hail Mary...

He was mindful of his covenant, and he showed compassion according to the multitude of his steadfast love. And he provided for them with mercies, in the sight of all those who had seized them. (Ps 106:44-45)
Hail Mary...

He has satisfied the thirsty, and he has satisfied the hungry soul with good things. (Ps 107:9)
Hail Mary...

They cried out to the Lord in their tribulation, and he freed them from their distress. And he led them out of darkness and the shadow of death, and he broke apart their chains. (Ps 107:13-14)
Hail Mary...

They cried out to the Lord in their tribulation, and he delivered them in their necessity. He sent his word, and he healed them, and he rescued them from their utter destruction. (Ps 107:19-20)
Hail Mary...

Glory Be…

Decade 2

Our Father…

But as for you, Lord, O Lord: act on my behalf for your name's sake. For your mercy is sweet. Free me, for I am destitute and poor, and my heart has been disquieted within me. (Ps 109:21-22)
Hail Mary...

He has created a memorial to his wonders; he is a merciful and compassionate Lord. He has given food to those who fear him. He will be mindful of his covenant in every age. (Ps 111:4-5)
Hail Mary...

Happy is the man who fears the Lord, who will delight in his commandments exceedingly. His offspring will be powerful on the earth. The generation of the upright will be blessed. Glory and wealth will be in his house, and his justice shall remain from age to age. (Ps 112:1-3)
Hail Mary...

The righteous one will be an everlasting memorial. He will not fear a report of disasters. his heart is firm, trusting in the Lord. (Ps 112:6-7)
Hail Mary...

He gives the barren woman to live in a house, makes her the joyful mother of children. (Ps 113:9)
Hail Mary...

The Lord has been mindful of us, and he has blessed us. He has blessed the house of Israel. He has blessed the house of Aaron. He has blessed all who fear the Lord, the small with the great. (Ps 115:12-13)
Hail Mary...

May the Lord add blessings upon you: upon you, and upon your children. May you be blessed by the Lord, who made heaven and earth. (Ps 115:14-15)
Hail Mary...

The Lord is my helper. I will not fear what man can do to me. (Ps 118:6)
Hail Mary...

The Lord is my strength and my praise. And he has become my salvation. (Ps 118:14)
Hail Mary...

I shall not die, but live, and declare the works of the Lord. (Ps 118:17)
Hail Mary...

Glory Be...

Decade 3

Our Father...

This is the day that the Lord has made. Let us rejoice and be glad in it. (Ps 118:24)
Hail Mary...

Blessed are the immaculate in the way, who walk in the law of the Lord. Blessed are those who keep his decrees, who seek him with their whole heart. (Ps 119:1-2)
Hail Mary...

How can young people keep their way pure? By taking heed according to your word. (Ps 119:9)
Hail Mary...

I have hidden your word in my heart, so that I may not sin against you. (Ps 119:11)
Hail Mary...

My soul has slumbered because of sorrow. Strengthen me in your words. (Ps 119:28)
Hail Mary...

I will always keep your law, in this age and forever and ever. I shall walk at liberty, because I was seeking your commandments. (Ps 119:44-45)
Hail Mary...

Remember your word to your servant, by which you have given me hope. This is my comfort in my distress: for your promises gives me life. (Ps 119:49-50)
Hail Mary...

I called to mind your ordinances of old, O Lord, and I was consoled. (Ps 119:52)
Hail Mary...

It is good for me that you humbled me, so that I may learn your statutes. (Ps 119:71)
Hail Mary...

If your law had not been my joy, then perhaps I would have perished in my misery. (Ps 119:92)
Hail Mary...

Glory Be…

Decade 4
Our Father…

I will never forget your precepts: for by them you have kept me alive. (Ps 119:93)
Hail Mary...

By your commandment, you have made me wiser than my enemies. For it is with me always. I have more understanding than all my teachers. For your decrees are my meditation. (Ps 119:98-99)
Hail Mary...

I obtained understanding by your commandments. Because of this, I have hated every way of iniquity. (Ps 119:104)
Hail Mary...

Your word is a lamp to my feet and a light to my path. (Ps 119:105)
Hail Mary...

I have been altogether afflicted, Lord. Revive me according to your word. (Ps 119:107)
Hail Mary...

The revealing of your words gives light; it gives understanding to the simple. (Ps 119:130)
Hail Mary...

Direct my steps according to your promise, and let no iniquity have dominion over me. (Ps 119:133)
Hail Mary...

Tribulation and anguish have found me. Your commandments are my delight. (Ps 119:143)
Hail Mary...

I rise before dawn and cry for help. For in your words, I have hoped beyond hope. My eyes preceded the dawn for you, so that I might meditate on your promise. (Ps 119:147-148)

Hail Mary...

Those who love your law have great peace, and nothing can make them stumble. (Ps 119:165)
Hail Mary...

Glory Be...

Decade 5

Our Father...

Let my supplication come before you; deliver me according to your word. (Ps 119:170)
Hail Mary...

I have lifted up my eyes to the mountains; from where will help come to me. My help is from the Lord, who made heaven and earth. (Ps 121:1-2)
Hail Mary...

The Lord is your keeper, the Lord is your protection, at your right hand. The sun will not burn you by day, nor the moon by night. (Ps 121:5-6)
Hail Mary...

The Lord will guard you from all evil. He will guard your life. The Lord will guard your entrance and your exit, from this time and forevermore. (Ps 121:7-8)
Hail Mary...

Those who sow in tears shall reap with shouts of joy. When departing, they went forth and wept, sowing their seeds. But when returning, they will arrive with shouts of joy, carrying their sheaves. (Ps 126:5-6)
Hail Mary...

Unless the Lord has built the house, those who build it have labored in vain. Unless the Lord has guarded the city, he who guards it watches in vain. (Ps 127:1)
Hail Mary...

Blessed are all those who fear the Lord, who walk in his ways. For you will eat the fruit of the labors of your hands. Blessed are you, and it will be well with you. (Ps 128:1-2)
Hail Mary...

Your wife is like an abundant vine within your house. Your children are like young olive trees surrounding your table. Behold, so will the man be blessed who fears the Lord. (Ps 128:3-4)
Hail Mary...

May the Lord bless you from Zion, and may you see the good things of Jerusalem, all the days of your life. And may you see the children of your children. Peace be upon Israel. (Ps 128:5-6)
Hail Mary...

If you, O Lord, were to heed iniquities, who, O Lord, could persevere? For with you, there is forgiveness, so that you may be revered. (Ps 130:3)
Hail Mary...

Glory Be…

Day 8

Decade 1

Our Father…

Let Israel hope in the Lord. For with the Lord there is steadfast love, and with him there is bountiful redemption. And he will redeem Israel from all its iniquities. (Ps 130:7-8)
Hail Mary...

O Lord, my heart has not been exalted, and my eyes have not been raised up. Neither have I walked in greatness, nor in wonders beyond me. But I have calmed and quieted my soul, like one who has been weaned from his mother, so was I recompensed in my soul. (Ps 131:1-2)
Hail Mary...

It is he who remembered us in our low estate: for his steadfast love endures forever: And has redeemed us from our enemies: for his steadfast love endures forever. Who gives food to all flesh: for his steadfast love endures forever. O give thanks unto the God of heaven: for his steadfast love endures forever. (Ps 136:23-26)
Hail Mary...

On the day that I called upon you: heard me. You increased the strength of my soul. (Ps 138:3)
Hail Mary...

For the Lord is exalted, and he looks with favor on the humble. But the lofty he knows from a distance. (Ps 138:6)
Hail Mary...

If I wander into the midst of tribulation, you will revive me. For you extended your hand against the wrath of my enemies. And your right hand has accomplished my salvation. (Ps 138:7)
Hail Mary...

O Lord, you have examined me, and you have known me. You have known my sitting down and my rising up. You have understood my thoughts from afar. My path and my fate, you have investigated. And you have foreseen all my ways. (Ps 139:1-3)
Hail Mary...

Even before a word is on my tongue, you know it completely. Behold, O Lord, you have known all things: the newest and the very old. You have formed me, and you have placed your hand over me. (Ps 139:4-5)
Hail Mary...

Where will I go from your Spirit? And where will I flee from your presence? If I ascend into heaven, you are there. If I descend into Hell, you are near. (Ps 139:7-8)
Hail Mary...

It was you who formed my inward parts; you knit me together in my mother's womb. I praise you, for I am fearfully and wonderfully made. Wonderful are your works. (Ps 139:13-14)
Hail Mary...

Glory Be…

Decade 2

Our Father…

Your eyes did see my unformed substance; and in your book were written all the days that were made for me. (Ps 139:16)
Hail Mary...

Examine me, O God, and know my heart. Question me, and know my paths. And see if there might be in me the way of iniquity, and lead me in the way of eternity. (Ps 139:23-24)
Hail Mary...

In his sight, I pour out my prayer, and before him, I declare my tribulation. Though my spirit may become faint within me, even then, you have known my paths. (Ps 142:2-3)
Hail Mary...

Make me hear your steadfast love in the morning. For I have hoped in you. Make known to me the way that I should walk. For I have lifted up my soul to you. (Ps 143:8)
Hail Mary...

Teach me to do your will. For you are my God. Your good Spirit will lead me into the righteous land. (Ps 143:10)
Hail Mary...

Blessed is the Lord, my God, who trains my hands for the battle and my fingers for the war. My rock and my fortress, my stronghold and my deliverer, my protector and him in whom I have hoped: he subdues my people under me. (Ps 144:1-2)

Hail Mary...

Send forth your hand from on high: rescue me, and free me from the mighty waters. (Ps 144:7)
Hail Mary...

O Lord, all eyes hope in you, and you provide their food in due time. You open your hand, and you fill every living being with a blessing. (Ps 145:15-16)
Hail Mary...

The Lord is near to all who call upon him, to all who call upon him in truth. He will fulfill the desire of those who fear him, and he will heed their supplication and accomplish their salvation. The Lord watches over all who love him. (Ps 145:18-20)
Hail Mary...

The Lord preserves the strangers; he upholds the orphan and the widow. (Ps 146:9)
Hail Mary...

Glory Be...

Decade 3
Our Father...

He heals the brokenhearted and binds up their wounds. (Ps 147:3)
Hail Mary...

Praise the Lord, O Jerusalem. Praise your God, O Zion. For he has reinforced the bars of your gates. He has blessed your children within you. He has stationed peace at your borders, and he has satisfied you with the fat of the grain. (Ps 147:12-14)
Hail Mary...

The Lord is well pleased with his people, and he will exalt the humble unto salvation. (Ps 149:4)
Hail Mary...

The fear of the Lord is the beginning of wisdom. (Pro 1:7)
Hail Mary...

Listen, my son, to the discipline of your father, and forsake not the law of your mother, For they will be a graceful ornament on your head, and a pendant to your neck. (Pro 1:8-9)
Hail Mary...

Give heed to my reproof. Lo, I will offer my spirit to you, and I will reveal my words to you. (Pro 1:23)
Hail Mary...

For if you would call upon wisdom and bend your heart to prudence, if you will seek her like money, and dig for her as if for treasure, then you will understand the fear of the Lord, and you will discover the knowledge of God. (Pro 2:3-5)
Hail Mary...

The Lord bestows wisdom, and out of his mouth, understanding and knowledge. (Pro 2:6)
Hail Mary...

He will preserve the salvation of the righteous, and he will protect those who walk uprightly. (Pro 2:7)
Hail Mary...

My son, do not forget my law, but let your heart guard my precepts. For they shall set before you length of days, and years of life, and peace. (Pro 3:1-2)
Hail Mary...

Glory Be…

Decade 4
Our Father…

Trust in the Lord with all your heart, and do not depend upon your own insight. In all your ways, acknowledge him, and he himself will direct your steps. (Pro 3:5-6)
Hail Mary...

Do not seem wise to yourself. Fear God, and withdraw from evil. Certainly, it shall be health to your flesh, and refreshment to your body. (Pro 3:7-8)
Hail Mary...

Honor the Lord with your substance, and give to him from the first of all your fruits, and then your storehouses will be filled with abundance, and your presses shall overflow with wine. (Pro 3:9-10)
Hail Mary...

Do not discard the discipline of the Lord, and do not fall away when you are corrected by him. For whomever the Lord loves, he corrects, and just as a father does with a son, in whom he delights. (Pro 3:11-12)
Hail Mary...

Preserve wisdom and prudence. And so shall there be life in your soul and grace in your voice. Then you shall walk confidently in your way, and your feet will not stumble. When you sit down, you shall not fear. When you rest, your sleep also will be sweet. (Pro 3:21-24)
Hail Mary...

Do not fear unexpected terror, nor the power of the impious falling upon you. For the Lord will be at your side, and he will guard your feet from being caught. (Pro 3:25-26)
Hail Mary...

Listen, my son, and accept my words, so that years of life may be multiplied for you. (Pro 4:10)
Hail Mary...

My child, pay attention to what I say, and incline your ear to my words. Let them not recede from your eyes. Keep them within your heart. For they are life to those who find them and healing to all their flesh. (Pro 4:20-22)
Hail Mary...

My son, pay attention to my wisdom, and incline your ear to my understanding, so that you may guard your thinking, and so that your lips may preserve discipline. (Pro 5:1-2)
Hail Mary...

The Lord beholds the ways of man, and he considers all his steps. (Pro 5:21)
Hail Mary...

Glory Be…

Decade 5

Our Father…

My child, preserve the precepts of your father, and do not dismiss the law of your mother. Bind them to your heart unceasingly and encircle them around your throat. When you walk, let them keep step with you. When you sleep, let them guard you. (Pro 6:20-22)
Hail Mary...

The commandment is a lamp, and law is a light, and the reproofs of discipline are the way of life. (Pro 6:23)
Hail Mary...

My son, guard my words and conceal my precepts within you. Son, preserve my commandments, and you shall live. And keep my law as the pupil of your eye. Bind it with your fingers; write it on the tablets of your heart. (Pro 7:1-3)

Hail Mary...

I love those who love me. And those who seek me diligently shall find me. (Pro 8:17)
Hail Mary...

With me, are wealth and glory, superb riches and justice. For my fruit is better than gold and precious stones, and my progeny better than choice silver. (Pro 8:18-19)
Hail Mary...

He who finds me, finds life, and he will draw salvation from the Lord. But he who sins against me will wound his own soul. (Pro 8:35)
Hail Mary...

The fear of the Lord is the beginning of wisdom, and knowledge of holiness is prudence. (Pro 9:10)
Hail Mary...

The Lord will not afflict with famine the soul of the righteous. (Pro 10:3)
Hail Mary...

The blessing of the Lord is on the head of the righteous. But iniquity covers the mouth of the impious. (Pro 10:6)
Hail Mary...

The blessing of the Lord causes riches. Affliction will not be a companion to them. (Pro 10:22)
Hail Mary...

Glory Be...

Day 9

Decade 1

Our Father…

The fear of the Lord adds days. And the years of the impious will be shortened. (Pro 10:27)

Hail Mary...

The hope of the righteous shall be gladness: but the expectation of the wicked shall perish. (Pro 10:28)

Hail Mary...

Some distribute their goods freely, and they become wealthier. Others withhold unduly, and they are always in need. (Pro 11:24)

Hail Mary...

Whoever trusts in his riches will fall. But the just shall spring up like a green leaf. (Pro 11:28)

Hail Mary...

The evil are ensnared by the transgression of their lips, but the righteous escape from trouble. From the fruit of the mouth one is filled with good things. (Pro 12:13-14)

Hail Mary...

Whoever despises the word bring destruction on himself. but those who respect the commandment shall be rewarded. (Pro 13:13)

Hail Mary...

In the fear of the Lord is the faithfulness of strength, and there shall be hope for his children. (Pro 14:26)

Hail Mary...

The fear of the Lord is a fountain of life, so as to turn aside from the snares of death. (Pro 14:27)

Hail Mary...

A gentle tongue is a tree of life. But that which is immoderate will crush the spirit. (Pro 15:4)

Hail Mary...

The Lord is far from the wicked: but he will hear the prayers of the righteous. (Pro 15:29)

Hail Mary...

Glory Be...

Decade 2

Our Father...

Open your works to the Lord, and your intentions will be set in order. (Pro 16:3)
Hail Mary...

By mercy and truth, iniquity is redeemed. And by the fear of the Lord, one turns away from evil. (Pro 16:6)
Hail Mary...

When the ways of man will please the Lord, even his enemies will be at peace with him. (Pro 16:7)
Hail Mary...

The mind of man plans his way. But the Lord to directs his steps. (Pro 16:9)
Hail Mary...

The name of the Lord is a very strong tower. The righteous run to it and are safe. (Pro 18:10)
Hail Mary...

Whoever guards a commandment guards his own soul. But whoever is reckless in his ways will die. (Pro 19:16)
Hail Mary...

Whoever is merciful to the poor lends to the Lord. And he will repay him for his efforts. (Pro 19:17)
Hail Mary...

The fear of the Lord is unto life. And he shall linger in plentitude, without being visited by disaster. (Pro 19:23)
Hail Mary...

Some take pride in chariots, and some in horses, but we will call upon the name of the Lord our God. (Pro 20:4-5)
Hail Mary...

Do not say, "I will repay evil." Wait for the Lord, and he will free you. (Pro 20:22)
Hail Mary...

Glory Be...

Decade 3

Our Father…

The fruit of humility is the fear of the Lord, riches and glory and life. (Pro 22:4)

Hail Mary...

Whoever is inclined to mercy shall be blessed, for from his bread he has given to the poor. (Pro 22:9)

Hail Mary...

Let not your heart compete with sinners. But be in the fear of the Lord all day long. For you will have hope in the end, and your expectation will not be taken away. (Pro 23:17-18)

Hail Mary...

If your enemy is hungry, feed him. If he is thirsty, give him water to drink. For you will gather hot coals upon his head, and the Lord will reward you. (Pro 25:21-22)

Hail Mary...

He that hides his sins, shall not prosper: but he that shall confess, and forsake them, shall obtain mercy. (Pro 28:13)

Hail Mary...

Whoever works his land shall be satisfied with bread. But whoever pursues leisure will be filled with need. (Pro 28:19)

Hail Mary...

A greedy man stirs up strife, but the one who trusts in the Lord will be enriched. (Pro 28:25)

Hail Mary...

Where there is no prophecy, the people will be scattered. Yet truly, But happy is he who keeps the law. (Pro 29:18)

Hail Mary...

Every word of God proves true. He is a bronze shield to those who hope in him. (Pro 30:5)

Hail Mary...

If you desire wisdom, keep the commandments, and then God will offer her to you. (Wis 1:26)

Hail Mary...

Glory Be…

Decade 4

Our Father…

For if he is a true child of God, he will help him and deliver him from the hands of his adversaries. (Wis 2:18)

Hail Mary...

The souls of the just are in the hand of God and no torment of death will touch them. (Wis 3:1)

Hail Mary...

And though, in the sight of men, they suffered torments, their hope is full of immortality. Having been disciplined a little, they will be well compensated, because God has tested them and found them worthy of himself. (Wis 3:4-5)

Hail Mary...

Make my teaching your longing and desire, and you will be well instructed. (Wis 6:11)

Hail Mary...

Wisdom is radiant and unfading, and she is easily discerned by those who love her, and is found by those who seek her. She hastens to make herself known to those who desire her. One who rises early to seek her will have no difficulty, for she will be found sitting at the gate. (Wis 6:12-13)

Hail Mary...

Who will know your mind, unless you give them wisdom and send your holy spirit from on high? (Wis 9:17)

Hail Mary...

O how good and gracious, Lord, is your spirit in all things! Therefore, those who wander afield, you correct, and, as to those who sin, you counsel them and admonish them, so that, having abandoned malice, they may believe in you, O Lord. (Wis 12:1-2)

Hail Mary...

Indeed, if we sin, we are yours, knowing your greatness; but we will not sin, because we know that we are counted as yours. (Wis 15:2)

Hail Mary...

Indeed, neither herb nor poultice healed them, but your word, O Lord, which heals all. (Wis 16:12)

Hail Mary...

Your children, whom you loved, O Lord, might know that it is not the fruits of nature which feed men, but your word, which preserves those who believe in you. (Wis 16:26)

Hail Mary...

Glory Be...

Decade 5

Our Father...

For in all things, O Lord, you magnified your people, and honored them, and did not despise them, but at every time and in every place, you assisted them. (Wis 19:22)
Hail Mary...

God has given, to the man who is good in his sight, wisdom, and knowledge, and rejoicing. But to the sinner, he has given affliction and needless worrying, and the work of gathering and heaping, only to give to one who pleases God. (Eccl 2:26)
Hail Mary...

This is a gift from God: that every man to whom God has given wealth and resources, and to whom he has granted the ability to consume these, may enjoy his portion, and may find joy in his labors. (Eccl 5:19)
Hail Mary...

The fear of the Lord will delight the heart and will give joy and gladness and length of days. (Sir 1:12)
Hail Mary...

If you desire wisdom, observe the commandments, and then God will offer her to you. (Sir 1:26)
Hail Mary...

Endure steadfastly for God. Stay with God, and persevere, so that your life may be prosperous in the very end. (Sir 2:3)
Hail Mary...

Accept everything that will happen to you, and persevere in your sorrow, and have patience in your humiliation. For gold and silver are tested in fire, and those who are found acceptable are tested in the furnace of humiliation. Put your trust in God, and he will make straight your ways, and hope in him. (Sir 2:4-6)
Hail Mary...

Those who fear the Lord will not be unbelieving toward his Word. And those who love him will keep to his way. (Sir 2:15)
Hail Mary...

Those who fear the Lord will seek the things that are well-pleasing to him. And those who love him will be filled with his law. (Sir 2:16)
Hail Mary...

Children, listen to your father, and act accordingly that you may be saved. For God honors a father above his children and confirms the right of a mother over her children. (Sir 3:1-2)
Hail Mary...

Glory Be...

Day 10

Decade 1

Our Father…

Those who honor their father atone for sins. they store up riches who respect their mother. (Sir 3:3-4)
Hail Mary...

He who honors his father will live a long life and those who obey the Lord honor their mother. (Sir 3:6)
Hail Mary...

Kindness to a father will not be forgotten, and will be credited to you against your sins; in the day of your distress it will be remembered in your favor; like frost in fair weather, your sins will melt away. (Sir 3:14-15)
Hail Mary...

Perform your works in meekness, and you shall be loved beyond the glory of men. However great you may be, humble yourself in all things, and you will find grace in the presence of God. (Sir 3:17-18)
Hail Mary...

Set your thoughts on the precepts of God, and meditate entirely on his commandments at all times, and he himself will give you insight, and the desire of wisdom will be given to you. (Sir 6:37)
Hail Mary...

Reach out your hand to the poor, so that your atonement and your blessing may be perfected. (Sir 7:32)
Hail Mary...

The gift of God remains with the just man, and his advancement will have success unto eternity. (Sir 11:17)
Hail Mary...

God made man in the beginning, and left him in the power of his own choice. He added his commandments and precepts. If you choose you can keep the commandments and to act faithfully is a matter of your own choice. (Sir 15:14-15)
Hail Mary...

He has set water and fire before you: stretch forth your hand to whichever you choose. Before man is life and death, good and evil, that which he shall choose shall be given him. (Sir 15:16-17)
Hail Mary...

He set his eye upon their hearts, to reveal to them the greatness of his works, so that they might highly praise his holy name, and give glory to his wonders, so that they might declare the greatness of his works. In addition, he gave them knowledge and the law of life, as their inheritance. (Sir 17:7-9)
Hail Mary...

Glory Be…

Decade 2

Our Father…

The number of the days of men are as many as one hundred years. Like a drop of water in the ocean, so they are considered to be. And like a grain of sand on the shore, so do these few years compare to the days of all time. For this reason, God is patient with them, and he pours forth his mercy upon them. (Sir 18:9-10)
Hail Mary...

Before you judge, examine yourself. And then you will find forgiveness in the sight of God. (Sir 18:20)
Hail Mary...

Son, have you sinned? You should not add further sins. Then too, for your former sins, pray so that they may be forgiven you. (Sir 21:1)
Hail Mary...

Supplications from the mouth of the poor will reach all the way to the ears of God, and judgment will come to him quickly. (Sir 21:5)
Hail Mary...

Whoever hates correction is walking in the steps of a sinner. But whoever fears God will convert within his heart. (Sir 21:6)
Hail Mary...

Forgive your neighbor, if he has harmed you, and then your sins will be forgiven you when you pray. (Sir 28:2)
Hail Mary...

Let your treasure be in the precepts of the Most High, and it will benefit you more than gold. Store your alms in the hearts of the poor, and it will obtain help for you against all evil. (Sir 29:11-12)
Hail Mary...

Who has had the power to transgress, but did not transgress and to do evil and did not do it? His prosperity will be established. (Sir 31:10-11)
Hail Mary...

Whoever fears the Lord will accept his discipline. And whoever rises early to seek him will find a blessing. (Sir 32:14)
Hail Mary...

No evil will befall the one who fears the Lord. Instead, God will preserve him during temptation and will free him from evil again and again. (Sir 33:1)
Hail Mary...

Glory Be...

Decade 3

Our Father...

The spirit of those who fear God will live, for their hope is in him who saves them. (Sir 34:14-15)
Hail Mary...

Those who fear the Lord will tremble at nothing, and they will not be terrified. For he is their hope. (Sir 34:16)
Hail Mary...

The eyes of the Lord are upon those who fear him. He is a powerful Protector, a Firmament of virtue, a Shelter from the heat, and a Covering from the midday sun, a Guardian from offenses, and a Helper from falling, who exalts the soul and illuminates the eyes, and who gives health and life and blessing. (Sir 34:19-20)
Hail Mary...

Whoever observes the law multiplies offerings. It is an offering of well-being to attend to the commandments and to withdraw from all iniquity. (Sir 35:1-2)
Hail Mary...

Give to the Most High according to his gifts to you, and act with a good eye toward the creations of your hands. For the Lord gives recompense, and he will repay you seven times as much. (Sir 35:12-13)
Hail Mary...

He whose service is pleasing to God shall be accepted, and his prayer shall reach to the clouds. (Sir 35:20)
Hail Mary...

The prayer of him that humbles himself, shall pierce the clouds: and it will not rest till till reaches its goal: and it will not cease till the most High answers.
Hail Mary...

He has rendered to men according to their deeds, and the works of all, according to his thoughts. (Sir 35:24)
Hail Mary...

Concerning all things, pray to the Most High, so that he may direct your way in truth. (Sir 37:15)
Hail Mary...

In your infirmity, you should not neglect yourself, but pray to the Lord, and he will heal you. (Sir 38:9)
Hail Mary...

Glory Be…

Decade 4
Our Father…

God will not abandon his mercy, nor will he corrupt or abolish his own works. And he will not perish the stock of the descendants of his elect. And he will not destroy the offspring of him who loves the Lord. (Sir 47:22)
Hail Mary...

By the word of the Lord, he closed the heavens, and he brought down fire from heaven three times. (Sir 48:3)
Hail Mary...

They called upon the merciful Lord. And they spread their hands and lifted them up to heaven. And the holy Lord God quickly heeded their voice. He was not mindful of their sins, and he did not give them over to their enemies. (Sir 48:20)
Hail Mary...

I will give thanks to you, O Lord, O King, and I will praise you, O God my Savior. I will give thanks to your name: for you have been a helper and protector to me. (Sir 51:1-2)
Hail Mary...

I will praise your name unceasingly, and I will praise it with thanksgiving, for my prayer was heeded. And you freed me from destruction and you rescued me from the time of iniquity. (Sir 51:11)
Hail Mary...

Come now, let us argue it out, says the Lord. Then, if your sins are like scarlet, they shall be made white like snow; and if they are red like crimson, they shall become white like wool. (Is 1:18)
Hail Mary...

If you are willing, and you listen to me, then you will eat the good things of the land. But if you are not willing, and you provoke me to anger, then the sword will devour you. For the mouth of the Lord has spoken. (Is 1:19-20)
Hail Mary...

The Lord himself will grant to you a sign. Behold, a virgin will conceive, and she will give birth to a son, and his name will be called Immanuel. (Is 7:14)
Hail Mary...

You should not say 'It is conspiracy!' For all that this people speaks is a conspiracy. And you should not be frightened or alarmed with their fear. The Lord of hosts, him you shall regard holy. Let him be your dread, and let him be your fear. (Is 8:12-13)
Hail Mary...

Behold: I and my children, whom the Lord has given to me are signs and portents, in Israel, from the Lord of hosts, who lives on Mount Zion. (Is 8:18)
Hail Mary...

Glory Be…

Decade 5

Our Father…

The people who walked in darkness have seen a great light. A light has risen for the inhabitants of the region of the shadow of death. (Is 9:2)
Hail Mary...

They will rejoice before you, like those who rejoice at the harvest, like the victorious exulting after capturing the prey, when they divide the spoils. For you have prevailed over the yoke of their burden, and over the rod of their shoulder, and over the scepter of their oppressor. (Is 9:3-4)
Hail Mary...

For unto us a child is born, and unto us a son is given. And leadership is placed upon his shoulder. And his name shall be called: wonderful Counselor, mighty God, Everlasting Father, Prince of Peace. (Is 9:6)
Hail Mary...

His burden will be taken away from your shoulder, and his yoke will be taken away from your neck. (Is 10:27)
Hail Mary...

The Spirit of the Lord will rest upon him: the spirit of wisdom and understanding, the spirit of counsel and fortitude, the spirit of knowledge and piety. And he will be filled with the spirit of the fear of the Lord. He will not judge according to the sight of the eyes, nor reprove according to the hearing of the ears. (Is 11:2-3)
Hail Mary...

He will judge the poor with justice, and he will reprove the meek of the earth with fairness. And he will strike the earth with the rod of his mouth, and he will slay the impious with the spirit of his lips. (Is 11:4)
Hail Mary...

In that day, the root of Jesse will stand as a sign among the people, the Gentiles shall inquire of him, and his dwelling will be glorious. (Is 11:10)
Hail Mary...

I will give thanks to you, O Lord, because though you have been angry with me; but your anger has been turned away, and you have consoled me. (Is 12:1)
Hail Mary...

Behold, God is my savior, I will trust, and I will not be afraid. For the Lord is my strength and my might, and he has become my salvation. (Is 12:2)
Hail Mary...

You will draw water with gladness from the wells of salvation. And you will say in that day: "Praise the Lord, and call upon his name! Make his deeds known among the peoples! Proclaim that his name is exalted! (Is 12:3-4)
Hail Mary...

Glory Be…

Day 11

Decade 1

Our Father…

A throne will be established in steadfast love, and One shall sit upon it in truth, in the tabernacle of David, judging and seeking judgment, and quickly repaying what is right. (Is 16:5)

Hail Mary...

They will return to the Lord. And he will listen to their supplications, and he will heal them. (Is 19:22)

Hail Mary...

I will place the key of the house of David upon his shoulder. And when he opens, no one will close. And when he closes, no one will open. And I will fasten him like a peg in a trustworthy place. And he will be upon a throne of glory in the house of his father. (Is 22:22-23)

Hail Mary...

O Lord, you are my God! I will exalt you, and I will praise your name. For you have accomplished wonderful things. Your plan, from of old, is faithful. (Is 25:1)

Hail Mary...

He will cast down violently, on this mountain, the face of the chains, with which all peoples had been bound, and the net, with which all nations had been covered. He will violently cast down death forever. And the Lord God will take away the tears from every face, and he will take away the disgrace of his people from the entire earth. (Is 25:7-8)

Hail Mary...

Behold, this is our God! We have waited for him, and he will save us. This is the Lord! We have endured for him. We will exult and rejoice in his salvation. (Is 25:9)

Hail Mary...

You will keep him in perfect peace, whose mind is steadfast: because he trusts in you. (Is 26:3)

Hail Mary...

Thus says the Lord God, the Holy One of Israel: If you return and are quiet, you shall be saved. Your strength will be found in silence and in hope. (Is 30:15)
Hail Mary...

The Lord waits, so that he may take pity on you. And therefore, he will rise up to show mercy on you. For the Lord is the God of judgment. Blessed are all those who wait for him. (Is 30:18)
Hail Mary...

You shall weep no more. Mercifully, he will take pity on you. At the voice of your outcry, as soon as he hears, he will respond to you. (Is 30:19)
Hail Mary...

Glory Be…

Decade 2

Our Father…

Though the Lord may give you the bread of adversity, and the water of affliction, yet your teacher will not hide from you anymore. And your eyes will behold your teacher. (Is 30:20)
Hail Mary...

Your ears will listen to the word of one admonishing you behind your back: "This is the way! Walk in it! And do not turn aside, neither to the right, nor to the left." (Is 30:21)
Hail Mary...

Wherever you sow seed upon the earth, he will give rain to the seed. And bread from the grain of the earth will be very plentiful and full. In that day, the lamb will pasture in the spacious land of your possession. And your bulls, and the colts of the donkeys that work the ground, will eat a mix of grains like that winnowed on the threshing floor. (Is 30:23-24)
Hail Mary...

The light of the moon will be like the light of the sun, and the light of the sun will be sevenfold, like the light of seven days, in the day when the Lord will bind the wound of his people, and when he will heal the stroke of their scourge. (Is 30:26)
Hail Mary...

Like birds flying overhead, so will the Lord of hosts protect Jerusalem, protecting and freeing, passing over and saving it. (Is 31:5)
Hail Mary...

O Lord, take pity on us. For we have waited for you. Be our arm in the morning and our salvation in the time of trouble. (Is 33:2)
Hail Mary...

The one who walks in righteousness and speaks the truth, who casts out greed with oppression and shakes all bribes from his hands, who blocks his ears so that he may not listen to bloodshed, and closes his eyes so that he may not see evil. Such a one will live on high; the fortification of rocks will be his lofty place. His bread will be supplied and his water will be assured. (Is 33:15-16)
Hail Mary...

Strengthen the weak hands, and make firm the weak knees! Say to the fainthearted: "Take courage and fear not! Behold, your God will come with vengeance. God himself will come to save you." (Is 35:3-4)
Hail Mary...

The eyes of the blind will be opened, and the ears of the deaf will be cleared. Then the disabled will leap like a dear, and the tongue of the mute will be untied. (Is 35:5)
Hail Mary...

The waters have burst forth in the desert, and fountains in solitary places. And the wilderness will have a pool of water, and the thirsty land will have springs of water. (Is 35:6-7)
Hail Mary...

Glory Be…

Decade 3

Our Father…

I will protect this city, so that I may save it for my own sake. (Is 37:35)
Hail Mary...

I will cry out, like a young swallow. I will moan, like a dove. My eyes have been weary by gazing upward. O Lord, I am oppressed! Be my security. (Is 38:14-15)
Hail Mary...

Every valley will be exalted, and every mountain and hill will be brought low. And the crooked will be straightened, and the uneven will become level ways. (Is 40:4)
Hail Mary...

The grass has dried up, and the flower has fallen. But the Word of our Lord remains for eternity. (Is 40:8)

Hail Mary...

It is he that gives power to the weary, and strengthens them that are powerless. (Is 40:29)
Hail Mary...

Even the youth will faint and be weary, and young men will utterly fall. But they that wait on the Lord shall renew their strength. They will mount up with wings like eagles. They will run and not be weary. They will walk and not faint. (Is 40:30-31)
Hail Mary...

You, O Israel, are my servant, O Jacob, whom I have chosen, the offspring of my friend Abraham. For his sake, I have taken you from the ends of the earth, and I have called you from its distant places. And I said to you: "You are my servant. I have chosen you, and I have not cast you aside." (Is 41:8-9)
Hail Mary...

Do not fear, for I am with you. Do not be afraid, for I am your God. I will strengthen you, and I will help you, and with my victorious right hand, I will uphold you. (Is 41:10)
Hail Mary...

All who fight against you shall be confounded and ashamed. They will be as if they did not exist, and those who strive against you will perish. (Is 41:11)
Hail Mary...

You will seek them, and you will not find them. Those who rebel against you will be as if they did not exist. And those who make war against you will be like nothing at all. (Is 41:12)
Hail Mary...

Glory Be...

Decade 4

Our Father...

I am the Lord your God. I hold you by your right hand, and I say to you: Do not be afraid. I will help you. (Is 41:13)
Hail Mary...

Fear not. I will help you, says the Lord, your Redeemer, the Holy One of Israel. (Is 41:14)
Hail Mary...

I have established you like a new threshing sledge, having serrated blades. You will thresh the mountains and crush them. And you will turn the hills

into chaff. You will winnow them, and the wind will blow them away, and the whirlwind will scatter them. And you shall exult in the Lord; you shall rejoice in the Holy One of Israel. (Is 41:15- 16)
Hail Mary...

The poor and the needy are seeking water, but there is none. Their tongue has been dried up by thirst. I, the Lord, will heed them. I, the God of Israel, will not abandon them. (Is 41:17)
Hail Mary...

I will open rivers in the high hills, and fountains in the midst of the plains. I will turn the desert into pools of water, and the dry land into streams of water. (Is 41:18)
Hail Mary...

I will plant the cedar in a deserted place, with the thorn, and the myrtle, and the olive tree. In the desert, I will plant the pine, and the elm, and the box tree together, so that they may see and know, acknowledge and understand, together, that the hand of the Lord has accomplished this, and that the Holy One of Israel has created it. (Is 41:19-20)
Hail Mary...

The things that were former, behold, they have come to pass. And I also declare what is new. Before these things arise, I will cause you to hear about them. (Is 42:9)
Hail Mary...

I will lead the blind along a way which they do not know. And I will cause them to walk along paths with which they were unfamiliar. I will turn darkness into light before them, and crooked into straight. These things I have done for them. For I have not abandoned them. (Is 42:16)
Hail Mary...

Thus says the Lord who created you, O Jacob, and who formed you, O Israel: Do not be afraid. For I have redeemed you, and I have called you by your name. You are mine. (Is 43:1)
Hail Mary...

When you pass through the waters, I will be with you; and through the rivers, they shall not overflow you: when thou walk through the fire, you shalt not be burned; neither shall the flame consume you. (Is 43:2)
Hail Mary...

Glory Be...

Decade 5
Our Father...

Because you are precious and honorable in my eyes, I have loved you, and I will present men on behalf of you, and nations on behalf of your life. (Is 43:4)
Hail Mary...

Fear not, for I am with you. I will bring your offspring from the East, and I will gather you from the West. (Is 43:5)
Hail Mary...

Do not call to mind the former things, nor consider the things of old. Behold, I am accomplishing new things. And now, it will spring forth. With certainty, you will know them. I will make a way in the wilderness, and rivers in the desert. (Is 43:18-19)
Hail Mary...

The wild beasts of the field will glorify me, with the serpents and the ostriches. For I have brought waters to the wilderness, rivers to the desert, in order to give drink to my people, to my elect. This is the people whom I have formed for myself. They will speak my praise. (Is 43:20-21)
Hail Mary...

I am. I am the very One who wipes away your iniquities for my own sake. And I will not remember your sins. (Is 43:25)
Hail Mary...

Thus says the Lord, who made and formed you, and will help you: Do not be afraid, my servant and my most righteous, whom I have chosen. (Is 44:2)
Hail Mary...

I will pour out waters upon the thirsty ground, and rivers upon the dry land. I will pour out my Spirit upon your descendants, and my blessing upon your offspring. (Is 44:3)
Hail Mary...

Remember these things, O Jacob, O Israel. For you are my servant. I have formed you. You are my servant, O Israel. You will not be forgotten by me. (Is 44:21)
Hail Mary...

I have wiped away your iniquities like a cloud, and your sins like a mist. Return to me, because I have redeemed you. (Is 44:22)
Hail Mary...

I will go before you. And I will level the mountains. I will shatter the doors of bronze, and I will break apart the bars of iron. I will give you the treasures of darkness, and hidden riches of secret places, so that you may know that I am the Lord, the God of Israel, who calls your name. (Is 45:2-3)
Hail Mary...Glory Be...

Day 12

Decade 1

Our Father...

For the sake of Jacob, my servant, and Israel, my elect, I have even called you by your name. I have surnamed you, though you have not known me. (Is 45:4)

Hail Mary...

All ends of the earth, be converted to me, and you will be saved. For I am God, and there is no other. (Is 45:22)

Hail Mary...

In the Lord, all the offspring of Israel shall be justified and shall glory. (Is 45:25)

Hail Mary...

And even to your old age I am he; and even with your hairs will I carry you: I have made, and I will bear; I will carry, and will deliver you. (Is 46:4)

Hail Mary...

From the beginning, I announce the last things, and from the start, the things that have not yet been done, saying: My plan will stand firm, and my entire will shall be done. (Is 46:10)

Hail Mary...

I have spoken it, and I will also bring it to pass. I have purposed it, I will also do it. (Is 46:11)

Hail Mary...

Long ago, I announced the former things. They went forth from my mouth, and I have caused them to be heard. I did these things suddenly, and they were fulfilled. (Is 48:3)

Hail Mary...

For the sake of my name, I will take the face of my fury far away. And for the sake of my praise, I restrain it for you, lest you perish. (Is 48:9)

Hail Mary...

Thus says the Lord, your Redeemer, the Holy One of Israel: I am the Lord, your God, who teaches you for your own good, who guides you in the way that you should go. (Is 48:17)

Hail Mary...

If only you had paid attention to my commandments! Your prosperity would have been like a river, and your success would have been like the waves of the sea, and your offspring would have been like the sand, and the stock from your loins would have been like its stones. (Is 48:18-19)
Hail Mary...

Glory Be...

Decade 2

Our Father...

They did not thirst in the desert, when he led them out. He produced water from the rock for them. For he split the rock, and the waters flowed out. (Is 48:21)
Hail Mary...

The Lord has called me from the womb; from the womb of my mother, he has been mindful of my name. And he has appointed my mouth as a sharp sword. In the shadow of his hand, he has protected me. And he has appointed me as an elect arrow. In his quiver, he has hidden me. (Is 49:1-2)
Hail Mary...

I shall be glorious in the eyes of the Lord, and my God shall be my strength. (Is 49:5)
Hail Mary...

They will not hunger or thirst, nor will the heat of the sun beat down upon them. For the one who takes pity on them will lead them, and he will guide them by springs of waters. (Is 49:10)
Hail Mary...

Give praise, O heavens! And exult, O earth! Let the mountains give praise with jubilation! For the Lord has consoled his people, and he will take pity on his suffering ones. (Is 49:13)
Hail Mary...

Can a woman forget her infant, so as not to take pity on the child of her womb? But even if she would forget, still I shall never forget you. (Is 49:15)
Hail Mary...

Behold, I have engraved you on my hands. Your walls are always before my eyes. (Is 49:16)
Hail Mary...

Even the captives will be taken away from the strong, even what has been taken by the powerful will be saved. And truly, I will contend with those who contend with you, and I will save your children. (Is 49:25)

Hail Mary...

I will feed your oppressors their own flesh. And they will be drunk with their own blood, as with new wine. And all flesh will know that I am the Lord, who saves you, and your Redeemer, the Strong One of Jacob. (Is 49:26)
Hail Mary...

The Lord has given me a teacher's tongue, so that I would know how to uphold the weary with a word. Morning after morning he wakens my ear, so that I may heed him like a teacher. (Is 50:4)
Hail Mary...

Glory Be…

Decade 3

Our Father…

The Lord God is my helper. Therefore, I have not been disgraced. Therefore, I have set my face like a very hard rock, and I know that I will not be put to shame. (Is 50:7)
Hail Mary...

He who justifies me is near. Who will speak against me? Let us stand together. Who is my adversary? Let him approach me. Behold, the Lord God is my helper. Who is the one who would condemn me? Behold, they will all be worn away like a garment; the moth will devour them. (Is 50:8-9)
Hail Mary...

Do not be afraid of disgrace among men, and do not dread when they revile you. For the worm will consume them like a garment, and the moth will devour them like wool. But my deliverance will be forever, and my salvation will be from generation to generation. (Is 51:7-8)
Hail Mary...

Now, those who have been redeemed by the Lord will return. And they will arrive in Zion with praising. And everlasting rejoicing will be upon their heads. They will take hold of gladness and rejoicing. Sorrow and sighing will flee away. (Is 51:11)
Hail Mary...

It is I, I myself, who will comfort you. Why then would you be afraid of a mortal man who must die, a human who will wither like the grass? (Is 51:12)
Hail Mary...

The oppressed shall speedily be released, and that he should not die and go down to the pit, nor that his bread should fail. I am the Lord your God, that

divided the sea, whose waves roared: The Lord of hosts is his name. (Is 51:14-15)
Hail Mary...

Shake yourself from the dust! Arise and sit up, O Jerusalem! Loose the chains from your neck, O captive! (Is 52:2)
Hail Mary...

How beautiful upon the mountains are the feet of the messenger and the preacher of peace! announcing good and preaching salvation, (Is 52:7)
Hail Mary...

Be glad and rejoice together! For the Lord has consoled his people. He has redeemed Jerusalem. (Is 52:9)
Hail Mary...

For you will not go out in a tumult, nor will you take flight in a hurry. For the Lord will go before you, and the God of Israel will be your rear guard. (Is 52:12)
Hail Mary...

Glory Be...

Decade 4
Our Father...

He himself was wounded because of our iniquities. He was bruised because of our wickedness. The discipline of our peace was upon him. And by his wounds, we are healed. (Is 53:5)
Hail Mary...

Enlarge the place of your tent and extend the curtains of your habitations, unsparingly. Lengthen your cords, and strengthen your stakes. For you shall extend to the right and to the left. And your offspring shall inherit the nations, and you shall inhabit the desolate cities. (Is 54:1-2)
Hail Mary...

Do not be afraid! For you will not be ashamed. Do not be discouraged, for you will not be put to disgrace. (Is 54:4)
Hail Mary...

For a brief moment, I have forsaken you, and with great pities, I will gather you. In a moment of indignation, I have hidden my face from you. But with everlasting mercy, I have taken pity on you, said your Redeemer, the Lord. (Is 54:7-8)
Hail Mary...

For the mountains will be moved, and the hills be removed. But my steadfast love will not depart from you.(Is 54:10)
Hail Mary...

O afflicted ones, convulsed by the tempest, away from any consolation! Behold, I will set your stones in order, and I will lay your foundation with sapphires, and I will make your ramparts out of jasper, and your gates out of sculpted stones, and all your borders out of desirable stones. (Is 54:11-12)
Hail Mary...

All your children will be taught by the Lord. And great will be the prosperity of your children. (Is 54:13)
Hail Mary...

You will be established in righteousness. You shall be far from oppression, for you will not be afraid. And from terror, for it will not come near you. (Is 54:14)
Hail Mary...

No weapon which has been formed to use against you will succeed. And every tongue that shall rise against you in judgment, you shall confute. (Is 54:17)
Hail Mary...

Why do you spend money for what is not bread, and expend your labor for what does not satisfy? Listen very closely to me, and eat what is good, and then your soul will be delighted by a full measure. (Is 55:2)
Hail Mary...

Glory Be…

Decade 5

Our Father…

Incline your ear and draw near to me. Listen, so that you may live. And I will make an everlasting covenant with you. (Is 55:3)
Hail Mary...

Behold, you will call to a nation that you did not know. And nations that did not know you will rush to you, because of the Lord your God, the Holy One of Israel. For he has glorified you. (Is 55:5)
Hail Mary...

Seek the Lord, while he may be found. Call upon him, while he is near. (Is 55:6)
Hail Mary...

Let the wicked one abandon his way, and the unrighteous man his thoughts, and let him return to the Lord, and he will have mercy on him, and to our God, for he is great in forgiveness. (Is 55:7)
Hail Mary...

My thoughts are not your thoughts, and your ways are not my ways, says the Lord. For just as the heavens are exalted above the earth, so also are my ways exalted above your ways, and my thoughts above your thoughts. (Is 55:8-9)
Hail Mary...

As rain and snow descend from heaven, and do not return there until they have soaked the earth, and watered it, and causing it to bloom and to provide seed to the sower and bread to the hungry, so also will my word be, which will go forth from my mouth. It will not return to me empty, but it will accomplish whatever I purpose, and it will succeed in the tasks for which I sent it. (Is 55:10-11)
Hail Mary...

They will keep my Sabbaths, and they will choose the things that pleases me, and they will hold to my covenant. I will give them a place in my house, within my walls, and a name better than sons and daughters. I will give them an everlasting name, which will never perish. (Is 56:4-5)
Hail Mary...

All who keep the Sabbath without profaning it, and who hold to my covenant. I will lead them to my holy mountain, and I will gladden them in my house of prayer. (Is 56:7)
Hail Mary...

He who takes refuge in me will inherit the earth and will possess my holy mountain. (Is 57:13)
Hail Mary...

This is said by the Most High, the Sublime One, who dwells in eternity. And his name is Holy, for he dwells in the exalted and holy place, and also with the contrite and humble spirit, to revive the spirit of the humble, and to revive the heart of the contrite. (Is 57:15)
Hail Mary...

Glory Be…

Day 13

Decade 1

Our Father…

I will not continuously accuse, and I will not be angry always. For then the spirits would become faint before me, even the souls that I have made. (Is 57:16)

Hail Mary...

I saw their ways, and I will heal them, and I will lead them back again, and I will restore consolations to them and to those who mourn for them, I will create the fruit of the lips: peace, peace to them who are far away, and peace to them who are near, says the Lord, and I will heal them. (Is 57:18-19)

Hail Mary...

Your justifier shall go before you, the glory of the Lord shall be your rear guard. (Is 58:8)

Hail Mary...

When you pour out your life for the hungry, and you satisfy the afflicted soul, then your light will rise up in darkness, and your darkness will be like the midday. (Is 58:10)

Hail Mary...

The Lord shall guide you continually, and satisfy your need in drought, and make strong your bones: and you shall be like a watered garden, and like a spring of water, whose waters never fail. (Is 58:11)

Hail Mary...

If you restrain from trampling the Sabbath, from doing your own will on my holy day, and if you call the Sabbath delightful, and the Holy of the Lord glorious, and if you glorify him, while you do not act according to your own ways, and your own will is not found, not even to speak a word, then you will find delight in the Lord, and I will take you up, above the heights of the earth, and I will nourish you with the inheritance of Jacob, your father. (Is 58:13-14)

Hail Mary...

Those from the west will fear the name of the Lord, and those from the rising of the sun will fear his glory, when he arrives like a violent river, which the Spirit of the Lord drives on. (Is 59:19)

Hail Mary...

This is my covenant with them, says the Lord. My Spirit is within you, and my words, which I have put in your mouth, will not withdraw from your mouth, nor from the mouth of your offspring, nor from the mouth of your offspring's offspring, says the Lord, from this moment, and even forever. (Is 59:21)
Hail Mary...

Arise, shine; for your light has come, O Jerusalem! For your light has arrived, and the glory of the Lord has risen over you. For behold, darkness will cover the earth, and thick darkness will cover the peoples. Then the Lord will rise above you, and his glory will be seen in you. And the nations will walk in your light, and the kings will walk by the splendor of your rising. (Is 60:1-3)
Hail Mary...

Lift up your eyes all around and see! All these have been gathered together; they come to you. Your sons will arrive from far away, and your daughters will rise up from your side. Then you will see, and you will be radiant, and your heart will rejoice and be amazed. (Is 60:4-5)
Hail Mary...

Glory Be...

Decade 2

Our Father...

The Spirit of the Lord is upon me, for the Lord has anointed me. He has sent me to bring good news to the meek, so as to heal the contrite of heart, to preach leniency to captives and release to the confined, and so to proclaim the acceptable year of the Lord and the day of vindication of our God: to console all who are mourning. (Is 61:1-2)
Hail Mary...

The Spirit of the Lord is upon me, for the Lord has anointed me....to take up the mourners of Zion and to give them a crown in place of ashes, an oil of joy in place of mourning, a cloak of praise in place of a spirit of grief. And there, they shall be called the strong ones of justice, the planting of the Lord, unto glorification. (Is 61:1,3)
Hail Mary...

Because their shame was double, and dishonor was proclaimed as their lot, they will possess double in their land. Everlasting joy will be for them. (Is 61:7)
Hail Mary...

I will turn their work into truth, and I will forge a perpetual covenant with them. Their descendants shall be known among the nations, and their

offspring in the midst of the peoples. All who see them will recognize them: that these are the people whom the Lord has blessed. (Is 61:8-9)
Hail Mary...

I will rejoice greatly in the Lord, and my soul will exult in my God. For he has clothed me with the vestments of salvation, and he has wrapped me in the clothing of justice, like a groom arrayed with a crown, and like a bride adorned with her jewels. (Is 61:10)
Hail Mary...

For as the young man will marry a young woman, so shall your maker marry you. And as the groom will rejoice over the bride, so shall your God rejoice over you. (Is 62:5)
Hail Mary...

The Lord has sworn with his right hand and with the arm of his strength: "Certainly, I will no longer permit your grain to be the food of your enemies. And foreigners will not drink your wine, for which you have labored. (Is 62:8-9)
Hail Mary...

Throughout all their tribulation, he was not troubled, It was no messenger or angel but his presence that saved them. With his love, and by his mercy, he has redeemed them, and he has carried them and lifted them up, throughout all the days of old. (Is 63:9)
Hail Mary...

Like an animal who descends to an open field, the Spirit of the Lord gave them rest. Thus did you lead your people, in order to make a glorious name for yourself. (Is 63:14)
Hail Mary...

From ages past, they have not heard it, and they have not perceived it with the ears. Apart from you, O God, the eye has not seen what you have prepared for those who wait for you. (Is 64:4)
Hail Mary...

Glory Be…

Decade 3

Our Father…

For behold, I am about to create the new heavens and the new earth. And the former things will not be in memory and will not enter into the heart. But you will be glad and exult, even forever, in these things that I create. For behold, I create Jerusalem as an exultation, and its people as a joy. (Is 65:17-18)

Hail Mary...

I will exult in Jerusalem, and I will rejoice in my people. And neither a voice of weeping, nor a cry of distress, will be heard in her anymore. (Is 65:19)
Hail Mary...

There will no longer be an infant who lives only a few days, nor an elder who does not complete his days. for one who dies at a hundred years will be considered a youth . (Is 65:20)
Hail Mary...

They will build houses, and will inhabit them. And they will plant vineyards, and will eat their fruits. (Is 65:21)
Hail Mary...

My elect will not labor in vain, and they will not bring forth in disorder. For they are the offspring of the blessed of the Lord, and their posterity are with them. And this shall be: before they call out, I will answer; while they are still speaking, I will hear. (Is 65:23-24)
Hail Mary...

My hand has made all these things, and all these things have been made, says the Lord. But upon whom will I look with favor, except upon a humble person, who is contrite in spirit, and who trembles at my word? (Is 66:2)
Hail Mary...

In the manner of one whom a mother comforts, so will I comfort you. And you will be comforted in Jerusalem. (Is 66:13)
Hail Mary...

You will see, and your heart will be glad, and your bodies will flourish like a plant, and the hand of the Lord will be known to his servants. (Is 66:14)
Hail Mary...

I know their works and their thoughts. I am arriving, so that I may gather them together with all nations and languages. And they will approach, and they will see my glory. (Is 66:18)
Hail Mary...

For in like manner as the new heavens and the new earth, which I will cause to remain before me, says the Lord, so will your offspring and your name remain. And there will be month after month, and Sabbath after Sabbath. And all flesh will approach, so as to worship before me, says the Lord. (Is 66:22-23)
Hail Mary...

Glory Be...

Decade 4

Our Father…

Before I formed you in the womb, I knew you. And before you went forth from the womb, I sanctified you. And I made you a prophet to the nations. (Jer 1:5)
Hail Mary...

Behold, I have placed my words in your mouth. Behold, today I have appointed you over nations and over kingdoms, so that you may root up, and pull down, and destroy, and scatter, and so that you may build and plant. (Jer 1:9-10)
Hail Mary...

They will make war against you, but they will not prevail. For I am with you, says the Lord, so that I may deliver you. (Jer 1:19)
Hail Mary...

O Israel, if you would return, says the Lord, then be converted to me. If you remove your abominations from before my face, then you will not be shaken. And you will swear, 'As the Lord lives,' in truth and in judgment and in justice." And the Gentiles will bless him, and they will praise him. (Jer 4:1-2)
Hail Mary...

I will make my words in your mouth like fire and this people like wood, and it will devour them. (Jer 5:14)
Hail Mary...

Let us dread the Lord our God, who gives us the timely and the late rains, in their proper time, who guards the full measure of the yearly harvest for us. (Jer 5:24)
Hail Mary...

I have placed the shore as a limit for the sea, as an everlasting precept that it will not pass. And its waves will crash, but they will not prevail; and its waves will swell, but they will not go across. (Jer 5:22)
Hail Mary...

I have presented you as a tester and refiner among my people. And you will test and know their way. (Jer 6:27)
Hail Mary...

Thus says the Lord of hosts, the God of Israel: Make your ways and your intentions good, and I will live with you in this place. (Jer 7:3)
Hail Mary...

If you truly amend your ways and your doings, if you exercise judgment between a man and his neighbor, if you do not act with deceit toward the new arrival, the orphan, and the widow, and if you do not pour out innocent blood in this place, and if you do not walk after strange gods, which is to your own harm, then I will live with you in this place. (Jer 7:5-7)
Hail Mary...

Glory Be...

Decade 5

Our Father...

Listen to my voice, and I will be your God, and you will be my people. And walk in the entire way that I have commanded you, so that it may be well with you. (Jer 7:23)
Hail Mary...

Listen to my voice, and do all that I command you, and then you will be my people and I will be your God. So shall I uphold the oath which I swore to your fathers, that I would give them a land flowing with milk and honey, just as it is this day. (Jer 11:4-5)
Hail Mary...

Could any of the graven images of the Gentiles send rain? Or are the heavens able to give showers? Have we not hoped in you, the Lord our God? For you have made all these things. (Jer 14:22)
Hail Mary...

I discovered your words and I consumed them. And your word became to me as the gladness and joy of my heart. For your name has been invoked over me, O Lord, the God of hosts. (Jer 15:16)
Hail Mary...

If you will be converted, I will convert you. And you will stand before my face. And if you utter what is precious and not what is vile. You will be my mouthpiece. (Jer 15:19)
Hail Mary...

I will present you to this people as a strong wall of brass. And they will fight against you, and they will not prevail. For I am with you, so as to save you and to rescue you, says the Lord. (Jer 15:20)
Hail Mary...

I will free you from hand of those who are most wicked, and I will redeem you from the hand of the powerful. (Jer 15:21)
Hail Mary...

Blessed is the man who trusts in the Lord, for the Lord will be his trust. And he will be like a tree planted beside waters, which sends out its roots to moist soil. And it will not fear when the heat arrives. And its leaves will be green. And in the time of drought, it will not be anxious, nor will it cease at any time to bear fruit. (Jer 17:7-8)
Hail Mary...

I am the Lord, who examines the heart and tests the mind, who gives to each one according to his way and according to the fruit of his own doings. (Jer 17:9-10)
Hail Mary...

Heal me, O Lord, and I will be healed. Save me, and I will be saved. For you are my praise. (Jer 17:14)
Hail Mary...

Glory Be...

Day 14

Decade 1

Our Father…

Thus says the Lord: Behold, I set before you the way of life and the way of death. (Jer 21:8)

Hail Mary…

I will gather together the remnant of my flock from the entire earth, from the places to which I had cast them out. And I will return them to their own fold. And they will increase and be multiplied. (Jer 23:3)

Hail Mary…

Behold, the days are approaching, says the Lord, when I will raise up to David a righteous branch. And a king will reign, and he will be wise. And he will exercise judgment and justice upon the earth. (Jer 23:5)

Hail Mary…

In those days, Judah will be saved, and Jerusalem will live in confidence. And this is the name that they will call him: 'The Lord is our righteousness.' (Jer 23:6)

Hail Mary…

Is not my word like fire, says the Lord, and like a hammer that breaks a rock in pieces? (Jer 23:29)

Hail Mary…

I will give them a heart, so that they may know me, that I am the Lord. And they will be my people, and I will be their God. For they shall return to me with their whole heart. (Jer 24:7)

Hail Mary…

Turn now, each one from his evil way, and from your wicked thoughts. And you shall dwell in the land, which the Lord has given to you and to your ancestors, from ancient times and even forever. (Jer 25:5)

Hail Mary…

Now, therefore, amend your ways and your intentions good, and heed the voice of the Lord your God. And then the Lord will change his mind of the evil that he has spoken against you. (Jer 26:13)

Hail Mary…

I know the plans that I have for you, says the Lord, plans of your welfare, and not for evil, to give you a future of hope. (Jer 29:11)
Hail Mary...

When you shall call upon me and come and pray to me, I will heed you. (Jer 29:12)
Hail Mary...

Glory Be…

Decade 2

Our Father…

When you seek me, you will find me; if you have sought me with your whole heart, I will be found by you, says the Lord. And I will restore your fortunes and gather you from all the nations where I have driven you. (Jer 29:13-14)
Hail Mary...

When the day comes, says the Lord of hosts: I will crush the yoke from their neck, and I will break open their chains. And foreigners will no longer rule over them. Instead, they will serve the Lord their God. (Jer 30:8-9)
Hail Mary...

Therefore, O my servant Jacob, you should not be afraid, says the Lord, and you should not be frightened, O Israel. For behold, I will save you from a far away land, and your offspring from the land of their captivity. (Jer 30:10)
Hail Mary...

I am with you, says the Lord, to save you: for I will utterly consume all the nations, among which I have scattered you: but I will not utterly consume you: but I will chastise you in just measure. (Jer 30:11)
Hail Mary..

All those who devour you, will be devoured. And all your enemies will be led into captivity. And those who devastate you, will be devastated. And all those who prey upon you, I will offer as a prey. (Jer 30:16)
Hail Mary...

I will close up your scar, and I will heal you of your wounds, says the Lord. (Jer 30:17)
Hail Mary...

I have loved you with an everlasting love: therefore I have drawn you with my faithfulness. (Jer 31:3)
Hail Mary...

They will approach with weeping. And I will lead them back with consolations. And I will lead them through the torrents of water, by an upright way, and they will not stumble in it. For I have become a father to Israel, and Ephraim is my firstborn. (Jer 31:9)
Hail Mary...

The Lord has redeemed Jacob, and he has freed him from the hand of one more powerful. (Jer 31:11)
Hail Mary...

They will arrive and give praise on Mount Zion. Then the virgin will rejoice with singing, the young and the old together, and I will turn their mourning into gladness, and I will console them and gladden them after their sorrow. (Jer 31:12-13)
Hail Mary...

Glory Be…

Decade 3

Our Father…

They will return from the land of the enemy. And there is hope for your very end, says the Lord. And your children will return to their own land. (Jer 31:16-17)
Hail Mary...

I will satisfy the weary, and I will replenish all who are faint. Therefore I awoke, and looked; and my sleep was pleasant unto me. (Jer 31:25-26)
Hail Mary...

This will be the covenant that I will form with the house of Israel, after those days, says the Lord: I will put my law in their inner most being, and I will write it upon their heart. And I will be their God, and they shall be my people. (Jer 31:33)
Hail Mary...

I will forgive their iniquity, and I will no longer remember their sin. (Jer 31:34)
Hail Mary...

O Lord God! Behold, you have made heaven and earth, by your great strength and by your outstretched arm. Nothing is too difficult for you. (Jer 32:17)
Hail Mary...

You are great in counsel and mighty in deed. Your eyes are open upon all the ways of mortals, so that you may repay each one according to his ways and according to the fruit of his doings. (Jer 32:19)
Hail Mary...

Behold, I am the Lord, the God of all the living. Is anything be too difficult for me? (Jer 32:26)
Hail Mary...

I will form an everlasting covenant with them, and I will not cease to do good for them. And I will put my fear into their heart, so that they do not withdraw from me. (Jer 32:40)
Hail Mary...

Call to me and I will answer you. And I will announce to you great and mighty things, that you do not know. (Jer 33:3)
Hail Mary...

Behold, I will lead over them recovery and health, and I will cure them. And I will reveal to them an abundance of prosperity and security. (Jer 33:6)
Hail Mary...

Glory Be…

Decade 4
Our Father…

I will cleanse them from all their iniquity, by which they have sinned against me. And I will forgive all their iniquities, by which they have offended against me and have despised me. (Jer 33:8)
Hail Mary...

Convert, each one from his wicked way, and make your intentions good. And do not choose to follow strange gods, nor shall you worship them. And then you shall live in the land which I gave to you and to your ancestors. (Jer 35:15)
Hail Mary...

I will free you in that day. And you will not be delivered into the hands of the men whom you dread. But when delivering, I will free you. And you will not fall by the sword. Instead, your life will be saved for you, because you had faith in me. (Jer 39:17-18)
Hail Mary...

As for you, my servant Jacob, you should not be afraid, and you should not dread, O Israel. For behold, I will bring your salvation from afar, and your offspring from the land of their captivity. (Jer 46:27)

Hail Mary...

As for you, my servant Jacob, do not be afraid, for I am with you. (Jer 47:28)
Hail Mary...

All who have seized them are holding them and refusing to release them. Their redeemer is strong. The Lord of hosts is his name. He will surely plead their case. (Jer 50:33)
Hail Mary...

Israel and Judah have not been forsaken by their God, the Lord of hosts, though their land has been filled with transgression against the Holy One of Israel. (Jer 51:5)
Hail Mary...

You are my weapon of war; and with you, I will strike together nations; and with you, I will scatter the kingdoms. (Jer 51:20)
Hail Mary...

If you had walked in the way of God, you would certainly have lived in everlasting peace. (Lam 3:13)
Hail Mary...

The steadfast love of the Lord never ceases, his mercies will never come to an end. They are new every morning: great is your faithfulness. (Lam 3:22-23)
Hail Mary...

Glory Be…

Decade 5
Our Father…

"The Lord is my portion," said my soul. Because of this, I will hope in him. The Lord is good to those who wait on him, to the soul that seeks him. It is good to stand ready in silence for the salvation of God. (Lam 3:25-26)
Hail Mary...

It is good for a man, to carry the yoke in his youth. He shall sit solitary and silent when the Lord has imposed it. He shall place his mouth in the dirt, perhaps there may be hope. (Lam 3:27-29)
Hail Mary...

For the Lord will not rebuke forever. For, if he has cast down, he will also have compassion, according to the multitude of his steadfast love. (Lam 3:31-32)
Hail Mary...

When the rights of a human are perverted in the presence of the Most High, when a person's cause is subverted—does the Lord not see it? (Lam 3:35-36)
Hail Mary...

Why would you forget us forever? Why would you forsake us for a long time? Restore us, O Lord, to you, and we shall be restored. Renew our days, as from the beginning. (Lam 5:20-21)
Hail Mary...

They will have a change of their heart in the land of their captivity, and they will know that I am the Lord their God. And I will give them a heart, and they will understand, ears, and they will hear. And they will praise me in the land of their captivity, and will remember my name. (Bar 2:31)
Hail Mary...

They will praise me in the land of their captivity and will remember my name. And they will turn themselves away from their stiff back, and from their wicked deeds, for they will call to mind the way of their fathers, who sinned against me. And I will restore them to the land which I pledged to their fathers, Abraham, Isaac, and Jacob, and they will rule over it, and I will multiply them, and they will not be diminished. (Bar 2:32-34)
Hail Mary...

You have accomplished in us, O Lord our God, according to all your kindness and according to all your great mercy. (Bar 2:27)
Hail Mary...

I will give them a heart, and they will understand, ears, and they will hear. And they will praise me in the land of their captivity and will remember my name. (Bar 2:31)
Hail Mary...

I will establish for them a new and everlasting covenant, so that I will be their God and they will be my people. And I will no longer move my people, Israel, out of the land which I have given them. (Bar 2:35)
Hail Mary...

Glory Be…

Day 15

Decade 1

Our Father…

O Lord Almighty, the God of Israel, listen now to the prayer of Israel and of their children, who have sinned before you and have not listened to the voice of the Lord their God, so that calamities have clung to us. Remember not the iniquities of our ancestors, but remember your power and your name at this time. (Bar 3:4-5)
Hail Mary...

You are the Lord our God, and we will praise you, O Lord. For you have imparted your fear into our hearts, and also, so that we may call upon your name and may praise you in our captivity. (Bar 3:6-7)
Hail Mary...

For if you had walked in the way of God, you would certainly have lived in everlasting peace. (Bar 3:12)
Hail Mary...

This is the book of the commandments of God and of the law, which exists in eternity. All those who keep it will attain to life, but those who have forsaken it, to death. (Bar 4:1)
Hail Mary...

Cry out to the Lord, and he will rescue you from the power and hand of the enemy. (Bar 4:21)
Hail Mary...

Be ever more peaceful in soul, for he who has named you, will comfort you. (Bar 4:30)
Hail Mary...

Look around, Jerusalem, towards the east, and see the joy that comes to you from God. (Bar 4:36)
Hail Mary...

Behold, your children approach, whom you sent away scattered. They approach, gathering together, from the east all the way to the west, at the word of the Holy One, rejoicing in the glory of God. (Bar 4:37)
Hail Mary...

Take off, O Jerusalem, the garment of your sorrow and affliction, and put on your beauty and the honor of that eternal glory, which you have from God. God will surround you with a double garment of righteousness, and he will set a crown on your head of everlasting honor. (Bar 5:1-2)
Hail Mary...

Arise, O Jerusalem, and stand in exaltation, and look around towards the east, and see your children, gathering together, from east to west, by the word of the Holy One, rejoicing that they are remembered by God. For they went out from you on foot, led by the enemies, but the Lord will lead them to you, being carried in honor like sons of the kingdom. (Bar 5:5-6)
Hail Mary...

Glory Be…

Decade 2

Our Father…

God has resolved to humble every high mountain and the longstanding cliffs, and to fill up the steep valleys in order to level the ground, so that Israel may walk diligently in the honor of God. (Bar 5:7)
Hail Mary...

My angel is with you, and he is watching over you. (Bar 6:7)
Hail Mary...

As for you, mortal, you should not fear them, and you should not dread their words. For you are among thorns and briers, and you are living with scorpions. You should not fear their words, and you should not dread their faces. (Eze 2:6)
Hail Mary...

If you announce to the righteous man, so that the righteous man may not sin, and he does not sin, then he shall certainly live, because you have announced to him. And you will have delivered your own soul. (Eze 3:21)
Hail Mary...

The Lord called to the man clothed in linen, who had the writing case at his side; and said to him, "Go through the city, through Jerusalem, and put a mark on the foreheads of those who sigh and groan over all the abominations that are committed in it." (Eze 9:3-4)
Hail Mary...

I will give them one heart. And I will put a new spirit within them. And I will take away the heart of stone from their body. And I will give them a heart of flesh. So may they may walk in my precepts, and observe my

judgments, and accomplish them. And so may they be my people, and I will be their God. (Eze 11:19-20)
Hail Mary...

I, the Lord, will speak. And whatever word I will speak, it shall be done, and it shall not be delayed any more. Instead, in your days, I will speak a word and do it, says the Lord God. (Eze 12:25)
Hail Mary...

I will remember my covenant with you in the days of your youth. And I will raise up for you an everlasting covenant. (Eze 16:60)
Hail Mary...

If the wicked man turns away from all his sins which he has committed, and if he keeps all my statutes, and does what is lawful and right, then he shall certainly live, and he shall not die. I will not remember all his iniquities, which he has committed; by his righteousness, which he has done, he shall live. How could it be my will that a wicked man should die, says the Lord God, and not that he should be converted from his ways and live? (Eze 18:21-23)
Hail Mary...

If the impious man does penance for all his sins which he has committed, and if he keeps all my precepts, and accomplishes judgment and justice, then he shall certainly live, and he shall not die. (Eze 18:27)
Hail Mary...

Glory Be…

Decade 3

Our Father…

I will judge each one according to his ways, says the Lord God. Be converted, and do penance for all your iniquities, and then iniquity will not be your ruin. Cast all your transgressions, by which you have transgressed, away from you, and make for yourselves a new heart and a new spirit. And then why should you die, O house of Israel? For I do not desire the death of one who dies, says the Lord God. So return and live. (Eze 18:30-32)
Hail Mary...

I also gave to them my Sabbaths, so that these would be a sign between me and them, and so that they would know that I am the Lord, who sanctifies them. (Eze 20:12)
Hail Mary...

I am the Lord your God. Walk in my precepts, and observe my judgments, and accomplish them. And hallow my Sabbaths, so that these may be a sign

between me and you, and so that you may know that I am the Lord your God.' (Eze 20:19-20)
Hail Mary...

Behold, I will kindle a fire in you, and I will burn up within you every green tree and every dry tree. The flame of the kindling will not be extinguished. (Eze 20:47)
Hail Mary...

As I live, says the Lord God, I do not desire the death of the impious, but that the impious should convert from his way and live. Be converted, be converted from your evil ways! For why should you die, O house of Israel? (Eze 33:11)
Hail Mary...

I myself will be the shepherd of my sheep, and I will make them lie down, says the Lord God. (Eze 34:15)
Hail Mary...

I will seek what had been lost. And I will lead back again what had been cast aside. And I will bind up what had been broken. And I will strengthen what had been infirm. (Eze 34:16)
Hail Mary...

I will make a covenant of peace with them. And I will banish the harmful beasts from the land. And those who are living in the wild will sleep securely. And I will make them a blessing all around my hill. (Eze 34:25-26)
Hail Mary...

The tree of the field will yield its fruit, and the land will yield its crop. And they will be secure in their own land. (Eze 34:27)
Hail Mary...

They will no longer be a prey to the Gentiles, nor will the wild beasts of the earth devour them. Instead, they will live in safety without any fear. (Eze 34:28)
Hail Mary...

Glory Be…

Decade 4
Our Father…

I will pour clean water over you, and you shall be cleansed from all your filth, and I will cleanse you from all your idols. And I will give to you a new heart, and I will place in you a new spirit. And I will take away the heart of stone from your body, and I will give to you a heart of flesh. (Eze 36:25-26)

Hail Mary...

I will place my Spirit within you so that you may walk in my precepts and keep my ordinances. (Eze 36:27)
Hail Mary...

I will save you from all your filth. And I will call for grain, and I will multiply it, and I will not impose a famine upon you. And I will multiply the fruit of the tree and the produce of the field, so that you may no longer bear the disgrace of famine among the nations. (Eze 36:29-30)
Hail Mary...

I will place my Spirit within you, and you shall live. And I will cause you to rest upon your own soil. And you shall know that I, the Lord, have spoken and acted, says the Lord God. (Eze 37:14)
Hail Mary...

They will no longer be defiled by their idols, and by their abominations, and by all their iniquities. And I will save them, out of all the places in which they have sinned, and I will cleanse them. And they will be my people, and I will be their God. (Eze 37:23)
Hail Mary...

I will strike a covenant of peace with them. This will be an everlasting covenant for them. And I will establish them and multiply them. I will set my sanctuary in their midst forevermore. And my tabernacle shall be among them. I will be their God, and they will be my people. (Eze 37:26-27)
Hail Mary...

The Gentiles shall know that I am the Lord, the Sanctifier of Israel, when my sanctuary will be in their midst forever. (Eze 37:28)
Hail Mary...

I will reveal my greatness and my holiness and I will be known in the eyes of the many nations. And they shall know that I am the Lord. (Eze 38:23)
Hail Mary...

I will make known my holy name in the midst of my people, Israel, and my holy name will no longer be defiled. And the Gentiles shall know that I am the Lord, the Holy One of Israel. (Eze 39:7)
Hail Mary...

May the name of the Lord be blessed by the present generation and forever; for wisdom and fortitude are his. He changes the times and the ages. He takes away kingdoms and he establishes them. He gives wisdom to those who are wise and teaching skills to those who understand. He reveals deep

and hidden things, and he knows what has been established in darkness. And the light is with him. (Dan 2:20-22)
Hail Mary...

Glory Be…

Decade 5
Our Father…

In the days of those kingdoms, the God of heaven will inspire a kingdom that will never be destroyed, and his kingdom will not be handed over to another people, and it will crush and will consume all these kingdoms, and this kingdom will stand in eternity. (Dan 2:44)
Hail Mary...

Do not hand us over forever, we ask you, because of your name, and do not abolish your covenant. And do not withdraw your mercy from us. (Dan 3:34-35)
Hail Mary...

We follow you wholeheartedly, and we fear you, and we seek your presence. Do not put us to shame, but deal with us in agreement with your patience and according to the multitude of your mercies. (Dan 3:41-42)
Hail Mary...

I watched until thrones were set up, and the Ancient one sat down. His garment was radiant like snow, and the hair of his head like clean wool; his throne was flames of fire, its wheels had been set on fire. A river of fire rushed forth from his presence. Thousands upon thousands ministered to him, and ten thousand times hundreds of thousands attended before him. The court sat in judgment, and the books were opened. (Dan 7:9-10)
Hail Mary...

I watched, therefore, in the vision of the night, and behold, with the clouds of heaven, one like a son of man arrived, and he approached all the way to the Ancient of days, and they presented him before him. And he gave him power, and honor, and the kingdom, and all peoples, tribes, and languages will serve him. His power is an eternal power, which will not be taken away, and his kingdom, one which will not be corrupted. (Dan 7:13-14)
Hail Mary...

For it is not through our righteousness that we offer our supplications before your face, but through the fullness of your compassion. (Dan 9:18)
Hail Mary...

"Fear not, O man of longing. May peace be with you. Take courage and be strong." And when he spoke to me, I was strengthened, and I said, "Speak, my lord, for you have strengthened me." (Dan 10:19)
Hail Mary...

Many of those who sleep in the dust of the earth will awaken: some to everlasting life, and others to a reproach and everlasting contempt. (Dan 12:2)
Hail Mary...

Those who are wise will shine like the brightness of the firmament, and those who instruct many towards justice, like the stars forever and ever. (Dan 12:3)
Hail Mary...

You have remembered me, O God, and you have not abandoned those who love you. (Dan 14:38)
Hail Mary...

Glory Be...

Day 16

Decade 1

Our Father…

I will betroth you to me forever, and I will betroth you to me in justice and judgment, and in mercy and compassion. And I will wed you to me in faith, and you will know that I am the Lord. (Hos 2:19-20)
Hail Mary...

The Lord loves the people of Israel, though they look to strange gods, and love the seeds of grapes. (Hos 3:1)
Hail Mary...

The Israelites will return, and they will seek the Lord their God and David their king, and they will come in awe to the Lord and by his goodness, in the last days. (Hos 3:5)
Hail Mary...

In their tribulation, they will arise early to me. Come, let us return to the Lord. For he has seized us, and he will heal us. He will strike, and he will cure us. He will revive us after two days; on the third day he will raise us up, and we will live in his sight. (Hos 6:1-3)
Hail Mary...

It was I who taught Ephraim to walk. I carried them in my arms. And they did not know that I healed them. I will draw them with the cords of kindness, with the bands of love. I picked them up and held them to my cheek and bent down to them and fed them. (Hos 11:3-4)
Hail Mary...

I will heal their disloyalty; I will love them spontaneously. For my wrath has been turned away from them. I will be like the dew; Israel will spring forth like the lily, and his root will spread out like that of the cedars of Lebanon. (Hos 14:4)
Hail Mary...

Who is wise and will understand this? Who has understanding and will know these things? For the ways of the Lord are right, and the upright will walk in them. (Hos 14:9)
Hail Mary...

But even now, be converted to me with your whole heart, in fasting and weeping and mourning. And rend your hearts, and not your garments, and convert to the Lord your God. (Joel 2:12-13)
Hail Mary...

Behold, I will send you grain and wine and oil, and you will again be filled with them. And I will no longer make you a mockery among the Gentiles. (Joel 2:18-19)
Hail Mary...

Do not be afraid. Exult and rejoice. For the Lord has great esteem for what he has done. Do not be afraid. For the beauty of the wilderness has sprung forth. For the tree has borne its fruit. The fig tree and the vine will give their full yield. (Joel 2:21-22)
Hail Mary...

Glory Be...

Decade 2
Our Father...

You, children of Zion, exult and rejoice in the Lord your God. For he will make the early and the late rains descend to you, just as it was in the beginning. And the threshing floors will be filled with grain, and the presses will overflow with wine and oil. (Joel 2:23-24)
Hail Mary...

I will repay you for the years which the locust, and the beetle, and the mildew, and the caterpillar consumed: my great strength which I sent upon you. (Joel 2:25)
Hail Mary...

You will eat with enjoyment, and you will be satisfied, and you will praise the name of the Lord your God, who has worked miracles with you. (Joel 2:26)
Hail Mary...

You will know that I am in the midst of Israel, and I am the Lord your God, and there is no other, and my people will not be put to shame forever. (Joel 2:27)
Hail Mary...

I will pour out my spirit upon all flesh, and your sons and your daughters will prophesy; your elders will dream dreams, and your youths will see visions. (Joel 2:28)
Hail Mary...

In those days I will pour out my spirit upon my servants and handmaids. And I will grant wonders in the sky and on earth: blood and fire and the vapor of smoke. (Joel 2:29-30)
Hail Mary...

Let the weak say, 'I am strong.' (Joel 3:10)
Hail Mary...

The Lord God does nothing revealing his secret to his servants the prophets. (Amos 3:7)
Hail Mary...

Seek good and not evil, so that you may live. And the Lord God of hosts will be with you, just as you have asked. Hate evil and love good, and establish judgment at the gate. Perhaps then the Lord God of hosts may have mercy on the remnant of Joseph. (Amos 5:14-15)
Hail Mary...

Behold, the days come, says the Lord, and I will send a famine on the earth: not a famine of bread, nor of thirst for water, but for hearing the word of the Lord. (Amos 8:11)
Hail Mary...

Glory Be…

Decade 3

Our Father…

I will turn back the captivity of my people Israel. And they will rebuild the deserted cities and inhabit them. And they will plant vineyards and drink their wine. And they will create gardens and eat their fruits. And I will plant them on their own soil. And I will no longer root them out of their own land, which I have given them, says the Lord your God. (Amos 9:14-15)
Hail Mary...

You are a gracious God, and merciful, slow to anger, and of great kindness, and ready to forgive. (Jon 4:2)
Hail Mary...

I will gather all of you, O Jacob. I will lead together as one, the survivors of Israel. I will set them together like a flock in the fold, like a sheep in the midst of the sheep pen. (Mic 2:12)
Hail Mary...

You, Bethlehem Ephrata, are a little one among the thousands of Judah. From you will go forth he who shall be the ruler in Israel, and his landing place has been set from the beginning, from the days of eternity. (Mic 5:2)

Hail Mary...

He will stand firm and feed his flock in the strength of the Lord, according to the majesty of the name of the Lord his God. (Mic 5:4)
Hail Mary...

Your hand will be exalted over your enemies, and all your adversaries will be cut off. (Mic 5:9)
Hail Mary...

I will look towards the Lord. I will wait for God, my Savior. My God will hear me. (Mic 7:7)
Hail Mary...

You, my enemy, should not rejoice over me. because when I fall, I will rise up, and when I sit in darkness, The Lord is my light. (Mic 7:8)
Hail Mary...

He will turn back and have mercy on us. He will put away our iniquities, and he will cast all our sins into the depths of the sea. (Mic 7:19)
Hail Mary...

The Lord is good, and a comforter in the day of tribulation, and he knows those who hope in him. He protects those who take refuge in him, even in a rushing flood. (Nah 1:7-8)
Hail Mary...

Glory Be…

Decade 4

Our Father…

Now I will shatter his yoke from your back, and I will break open the bonds that bind you. (Nah 1:13)
Hail Mary...

Though the fig tree will not flower, and there will be no bud on the vines. Though the labor of the olive tree will be misleading, and the farmland will produce no food. Though the sheep will be cut off from the sheepfold, and there will be no herd at the manger. But I will rejoice in the Lord; and I will exult in the God of my salvation. (Hab 3:17-18)
Hail Mary...

The Lord God is my strength. And he will set my feet like those of the deer. And he will lead me beyond my high places. (Hab 3:19)
Hail Mary...

The Lord their God will be mindful of them, and he will restore their fortunes. (Zeph 2:7)
Hail Mary...

I will change the speech of the people to a pure speech, that they may all call upon the name of the Lord, to serve him with one accord. (Zeph 3:9)
Hail Mary...

The Lord, your God, is in your midst, a warrior who gives victory; he will rejoice over you with gladness, he will renew you in his love; he will exult over you with loud singing. (Zeph 3:17)
Hail Mary...

Give praise, Shout joyfully. Rejoice and exult with all your heart. The Lord has taken away the judgments against you; he has turned aside your enemies. The king of Israel, the Lord, is in your midst; you shall no longer fear evil. (Zeph 3:14-15)
Hail Mary...

In that time, when I will bring you home, and in the time when I will gather for you. For I will make you into renown and into praise, among all the peoples of the earth, when I will restore your fortunes before your very eyes, says the Lord. (Zeph 3:20)
Hail Mary...

Thus says the Lord of hosts: Consider how you have fared. Ascend to the mountain, bring wood and build the house, and it shall be acceptable to me, and I shall be glorified, says the Lord. (Hag 1:7-8)
Hail Mary...

My Spirit is in your midst. Do not be afraid. (Hag 2:5)
Hail Mary...

Glory Be…

Decade 5

Our Father…

Thus says the Lord of hosts: Turn to me, says the Lord of hosts, and I will turn to you, says the Lord of hosts. (Zech 1:3)
Hail Mary...

I will be to it a wall of fire all around, says the Lord, and I will be the glory within it. (Zech 2:5)
Hail Mary...

Sing praise and rejoice, daughter of Zion. For behold, I come, and I will dwell in your midst, says the Lord. (Zech 2:10)
Hail Mary...

Not by might, nor by power, but in my spirit, says the Lord of hosts. (Zech 4:6)
Hail Mary...

Turn back to the fortress, prisoners of hope. Today, I announce that I will restore to you double. (Zech 9:12)
Hail Mary...

I will strengthen the house of Judah, and I will save the house of Joseph, and I will convert them, because I will have mercy on them. And they will be as they were when I had not cast them away. For I am the Lord their God, and I will hear them. (Zech 10:6)
Hail Mary...

For, from the days of your ancestors, you have withdrawn from my ordinances and have not kept them. Return to me, and I will return to you, says the Lord of hosts. (Mal 3:7)
Hail Mary...

Bring all the tithes into the storehouse, and let there be food in my house. And test me about this, says the Lord, as to whether I will not open to you the floodgates of heaven, and pour out to you a blessing, all the way to abundance. (Mal 3:10)
Hail Mary...

I will rebuke for your sakes the devourer, and he will not corrupt the fruit of your land. Neither will the vine in the field be barren, says the Lord of hosts. And all nations will call you blessed. For you will be a desirable land, says the Lord of hosts. (Mal 3:11-12)
Hail Mary...

Those who fear the Lord spoke, each one with his neighbor. And the Lord paid attention and heeded. And a book of remembrance was written in his sight, for those who fear the Lord and for those who consider his name. And they will be my special possession, says the Lord of hosts, on the day that I act. (Mal 3:16-17)
Hail Mary...

Glory Be…

Day 17

Decade 1
Our Father…

But unto you, who fear my name, the Sun of justice will arise, and health will be in his wings. And you will go forth and leap like the calves of the herd. (Mal 4:2)
Hail Mary…

You will trample the wicked, while they will be ashes under the sole of your foot, on the day that I act, says the Lord of hosts. (Mal 4:3)
Hail Mary…

Behold, a virgin shall conceive in her womb, and she shall give birth to a son. And they shall call his name Emmanuel, which means: God is with us. (Matt 1:23)
Hail Mary…

Man shall not live by bread alone, but by every word that proceeds from the mouth of God. (Matt 4:4)
Hail Mary…

Jesus traveled throughout all of Galilee, teaching in their synagogues, and preaching the Gospel of the kingdom, and healing every sickness and every infirmity among the people. (Matt 4:23)
Hail Mary…

Blessed are the poor in spirit, for theirs is the kingdom of heaven. Blessed are those who mourn, for they shall be consoled. Blessed are the meek, for they shall inherit the earth. (Matt 5:3-5)
Hail Mary…

Blessed are those who hunger and thirst for righteousness, for they shall be satisfied. Blessed are the merciful, for they shall receive mercy. Blessed are the pure in heart, for they shall see God. Blessed are the peacemakers, for they shall be called children of God. (Matt 5:6-9)
Hail Mary…

Blessed are those who endure persecution for the sake of righteousness, for theirs is the kingdom of heaven. (Matt 5:10)
Hail Mary…

Blessed are you when they have slandered you, and persecuted you, and spoken all kinds of evil against you, falsely, for my sake. Be glad and exult, for your reward in heaven is great. For in the same way they persecuted the prophets who were before you. (Matt 5:11-12)
Hail Mary...

You are the light of the world. So then, let your light shine in the sight of men, so that they may see your good works, and may glorify your Father, who is in heaven. (Matt 5:14,16)
Hail Mary...

Glory Be...

Decade 2

Our Father...

Until heaven and earth pass away, not one letter, not one stroke shall pass away from the law, until all is accomplished. (Matt 5:18)
Hail Mary...

Whoever breaks one of the least of these commandments, and teaches others to do the same, shall be called the least in the kingdom of heaven. But whoever does them and teaches others, such a one shall be called great in the kingdom of heaven. (Matt 5:19)
Hail Mary...

If you offer your gift at the altar, and there you remember that your brother has something against you, leave your gift there, before the altar, and go first to be reconciled to your brother, and then you may approach and offer your gift. (Matt 5:23-24)
Hail Mary...

Love your enemies. Do good to those who hate you. And pray for those who persecute and slander you, so that you may become the children of your Father in heaven. (Matt 5:44-45)
Hail Mary...

But when you give alms, do not let your left hand know what your right hand is doing, so that your almsgiving may be in secret, and your Father, who sees in secret, will repay you. (Matt 6:3-4)
Hail Mary...

But you, when you pray, enter into your room, and having shut the door, pray to your Father in secret, and your Father, who sees in secret, will repay you. (Matt 6:6)
Hail Mary...

When praying, do not choose many words, as the pagans do. For they think that by their excess of words they might be heard. Therefore, do not choose to imitate them. For your Father knows what your needs may be, even before you ask him. (Matt 6:7-8)
Hail Mary...

If you will forgive men their sins, your heavenly Father also will forgive you your offenses. But if you will not forgive men, neither will your Father forgive you your sins. (Matt 6:14-15)
Hail Mary...

But as for you, when you fast, anoint your head and wash your face, so that your fasting will not be seen by others, but by your Father, who is in secret. And your Father, who sees in secret, will repay you. (Matt 6:17-18)
Hail Mary...

Do not choose to store up for yourselves treasures on earth: where rust and moth consume, and where thieves break in and steal. Instead, store up for yourselves treasures in heaven: where neither rust nor moth consumes, and where thieves do not break in and steal. For where your treasure is, there your heart will be also. (Matt 6:19-21)
Hail Mary...

Glory Be…

Decade 3

Our Father…

The lamp of your body is your eye. If your eye is wholesome, your entire body will be filled with light. But if your eye has been corrupted, your entire body will be darkened. If then the light that is in you is darkness, how great will the darkness be! (Matt 6:22-23)
Hail Mary...

Do not worry about your life, as to what you will eat, nor about your body, as to what you will wear. Is not life more than food, and the body more than clothing? (Matt 6:25)
Hail Mary...

Consider the birds of the air, how they neither sow, nor reap, nor gather into barns, and yet your heavenly Father feeds them. Are you not of more value than they are? (Matt 6:26)
Hail Mary...

Can any of you, by worrying, add a single hour to your span of life? Why do you worry about clothing? Consider the lilies of the field, how they grow; they neither work nor weave. But I say to you, that not even Solomon, in all

his glory, was clothed like one of these. So if God so clothes the grass of the field, which is here today, and cast into the oven tomorrow, how much more will clothe you, O little in faith? (Matt 6:27-30)
Hail Mary...

Therefore, do not worry, saying: 'What shall we eat, and what shall we drink, and with what shall we be clothed?' For the Gentiles seek all these things. Indeed your Father knows that you need all these things. (Matt 6:31-32)
Hail Mary...

Seek first the kingdom of God and his righteousness, and all these things shall be added to you as well. (Matt 6:33)
Hail Mary...

Do not worry about tomorrow; for the future day will bring worries of its own. Today's trouble is enough for the day. (Matt 6:34)
Hail Mary...

Do not judge, so that you may not be judged. For with whatever judgment you judge, so shall you be judged; and with whatever measure you measure out, so shall it be measured back to you. (Matt 7:1-2)
Hail Mary...

Ask, and it shall be given to you. Seek, and you shall find. Knock, and it shall be opened to you. For everyone who asks, receives; and whoever seeks, finds; and to anyone who knocks, it will be opened. (Matt 7:7-8)
Hail Mary...

Or what man is there among you, who, if his son were to ask him for bread, would offer him a stone; or if he were to ask him for a fish, would offer him a snake? Therefore, if you, though you are evil, know how to give good gifts to your children, how much more will your Father, who is in heaven, give good things to those who ask him? (Matt 7:9-11)
Hail Mary...

Glory Be...

Decade 4
Our Father...

Therefore, all things whatsoever that you wish that others would do to you, do so also to them. For this is the law and the prophets. (Matt 7:12)
Hail Mary...

Enter through the narrow gate. For wide is the gate, and broad is the way, which leads to destruction, and there are many who enter through it. The

gate is narrow and straight is the way that leads to life, and few there are who find it! (Matt 7:13-14)
Hail Mary...

Not all who say to me, 'Lord, Lord,' will enter into the kingdom of heaven. But whoever does the will of my Father in heaven, shall enter into the kingdom of heaven. (Matt 7:21)
Hail Mary...

Everyone who hears these words of mine and does them shall be compared to a wise man, who built his house upon rock. The rains descended, and the floods rose up, and the winds blew, and rushed upon that house, but it did not fall, for it was founded on rock. (Matt 7:24-25)
Hail Mary...

A leper, drawing near, adored him, saying, "Lord, if you choose, you can make me clean." And Jesus, extending his hand, touched him, saying: "I am willing. Be cleansed." And immediately his leprosy was cleansed. (Matt 8:2-3)
Hail Mary...

Lord, I am not worthy that you should enter under my roof, but only say the word, and my servant shall be healed. (Matt 8:8)
Hail Mary...

Go; let it be done for you according to your faith. (Matt 8:13)
Hail Mary...

When evening arrived, they brought to him many who had demons, and he cast out the spirits with a word. And he healed all those having sicknesses. (Matt 8:16)
Hail Mary...

Jesus, turning and seeing her, said: "Be strengthened in faith, daughter; your faith has made you well." And the woman was made well from that hour. (Matt 9:22)
Hail Mary...

He touched their eyes, saying, "According to your faith let it be done for you." And their eyes were opened. (Matt 9:29)
Hail Mary...

Glory Be...

Decade 5
Our Father...

Behold, they brought him a man who was mute, having a demon. And after the demon was cast out, the mute man spoke. And the crowds wondered, saying, "Never has anything like this been seen in Israel." (Matt 9:32-33)
Hail Mary...

Jesus traveled throughout all of the cities and towns, teaching in their synagogues, and preaching the Gospel of the kingdom, and healing every illness and every infirmity. (Matt 9:35)
Hail Mary...

Seeing the multitudes, he had compassion on them, because they were distressed and helpless, like sheep without a shepherd. (Matt 9:36)
Hail Mary...

Having called together his twelve disciples, he gave them authority over unclean spirits, to cast them out and to cure every sickness and every infirmity. (Matt 10:1)
Hail Mary...

Cure the infirm, raise the dead, cleanse the lepers, cast out demons.(Matt 10:8)
Hail Mary...

Do not worry about how you are to speak or or what you are to speak. For what to speak shall be given to you in that hour. For it is not you who will be speaking, but the Spirit of your Father, who will speak through you. (Matt 10:19-20)
Hail Mary...

Do not be afraid of those who kill the body, but are not able to kill the soul. But instead fear him who is able to destroy both soul and body in Hell. (Matt 10:28)
Hail Mary...

Are not two sparrows sold for one small coin? And yet not one of them will fall to the ground without your Father. For even the hairs of your head have all been counted. Therefore, do not be afraid. You are worth more than many sparrows. (Matt 10:29-31)
Hail Mary...

Everyone who acknowledges me before men, I also will acknowledge before my Father, who is in heaven. But whoever will have denied me before men, I also will deny before my Father, who is in heaven. (Matt 10:32-33)
Hail Mary...

Whoever finds his life, will lose it. And whoever will have lost his life because of me, shall find it. (Matt 10:39) *Hail Mary...Glory Be...*

Day 18

Decade 1

Our Father…

Whoever receives you, receives me. And whoever receives me, receives him who sent me. (Matt 10:40)

Hail Mary...

Whoever receives a prophet, in the name of a prophet, shall receive the reward of a prophet. And whoever receives the righteous in the name of the righteous shall receive the reward of the righteous. And whoever shall give, even to one of the least of these, a cup of cold water to drink in the name of a disciple: Amen I say to you, he shall not lose his reward. (Matt 10:41-42)

Hail Mary...

Are not two sparrows sold for one small coin? And yet not one of them will fall to the ground apart from your Father. For even the hairs of your head are all counted. Therefore, do not be afraid. You are worth more than many sparrows. (Matt 10:29-31)

Hail Mary...

All things have been delivered to me by my Father. And no one knows the Son except the Father, nor does anyone know the Father except the Son, and those to whom the Son is willing to reveal him. (Matt 11:27)

Hail Mary...

Come to me, all you who labor and have been burdened, and I will give you rest. (Matt 11:28)

Hail Mary...

Take my yoke upon you, and learn from me, for I am meek and humble of heart; and you shall find rest for your souls. For my yoke is easy and my burden is light. (Matt 11:29-30)

Hail Mary...

Whoever is not with me, is against me. And whoever does not gather with me, scatters. (Matt 12:30)

Hail Mary...

For every idle word which men will have spoken, they shall render an account in the day of judgment. For by your words shall you be justified, and by your words shall you be condemned. (Matt 12:36-37)

Hail Mary...

Anyone who does the will of my Father, who is in heaven is my brother, and sister, and mother. (Matt 12:50)
Hail Mary...

Whoever has received the seed into good soil, this is he who hears the word, and understands it, and so he bears fruit, and he produces: some a hundred fold, and another sixty fold, and another thirty fold. (Matt 13:23)
Hail Mary...

Glory Be...

Decade 2

Our Father...

When the men of that place had recognized him, they sent into all that region, and they brought to him all who had sicknesses. And they petitioned him, so that they might touch even the hem of his garment. And as many as touched it were made whole. (Matt 14:35)
Hail Mary...

I say to you, that you are Peter, and upon this rock I will build my Church, and the gates of Hell shall not prevail against it. (Matt 16:18)
Hail Mary...

I will give you the keys of the kingdom of heaven. And whatever you shall bind on earth shall be bound, even in heaven. And whatever you shall release on earth shall be released, even in heaven. (Matt 16:19)
Hail Mary...

If anyone is willing to come after me, let him deny himself, and take up his cross, and follow me. (Matt 16:24)
Hail Mary...

Whoever would save his life, will lose it. But whoever will have lost his life for my sake, shall find it. (Matt 16:25)
Hail Mary...

Amen I say to you, certainly, if you will have faith like a grain of mustard seed, you will say to this mountain, 'Move from here to there,' and it shall move. And nothing will be impossible for you. (Matt 17:19-20)
Hail Mary...

Amen I say to you, unless you change and become like little children, you shall not enter into the kingdom of heaven. Therefore, whoever will have humbled himself like this little child, such a one is greater in the kingdom of heaven. (Matt 18:3-4)
Hail Mary...

See to it that you do not despise even one of these little ones. For I say to you, that their angels in heaven continually look upon the face of my Father in heaven. (Matt 18:10)
Hail Mary...

It is not the will of your Father, who is in heaven, that one of these little ones should be lost. (Matt 18:14)
Hail Mary...

Again I say to you, that if two of you have agreed on earth, about anything whatsoever that you have requested, it shall be done for you by my Father, who is in heaven (Matt 18:19)
Hail Mary....

Glory Be…

Decade 3

Our Father…

Wherever two or three are gathered in my name, there am I, in their midst. (Matt 18:20)
Hail Mary...

Then Peter, drawing near to him, said: "Lord, how many times shall my brother sin against me, and I forgive him? As many as seven times?" Jesus said to him: "Not just seven times, but I say to you, seventy times seven. (Matt 18:21-22)
Hail Mary...

Jesus said to them: "Allow the little children to come to me, and do not stop them. For the kingdom of heaven is among such as these." (Matt 19:14)
Hail Mary...

If you wish to enter into life, observe the commandments. (Matt 19:17)
Hail Mary...

With men, this is impossible. But with God, all things are possible. (Matt 19:26)
Hail Mary...

Amen I say to you, that at the resurrection, when the Son of man shall sit on the seat of his majesty, those of you who have followed me shall also sit on twelve seats, judging the twelve tribes of Israel. (Matt 19:28)
Hail Mary...

Anyone who has left behind home, or brothers, or sisters, or father, or mother, or wife, or children, or land, for the sake of my name, shall receive

one hundred times more, and shall possess eternal life. But many of those who are first shall be last, and the last shall be first. (Matt 19:29-30)
Hail Mary...

Amen I say to you, if you have faith and do not doubt, not only shall you do this, concerning the fig tree, but even if you would say to this mountain, 'Take and cast yourself into the sea,' it shall be done. (Matt 21:21)
Hail Mary...

All things whatsoever that you shall ask for in prayer with faith, you shall receive. (Matt 21:22)
Hail Mary...

Whoever has exalted himself, shall be humbled. And whoever has humbled himself, shall be exalted. (Matt 23:12)
Hail Mary...

Glory Be…

Decade 4
Our Father…

Many false prophets will arise, and they will lead many astray. And because iniquity has abounded, the love of many will grow cold. But whoever will have persevered until the end will be saved. (Matt 24:11-13)
Hail Mary...

For just as lightning goes out from the east, and appears as far as the west, so shall it be also at the advent of the Son of man. Wherever the corpse is, there the vultures gather together. (Matt 24:27)
Hail Mary...

Then the sign of the Son of man shall appear in heaven. And then all the tribes of the earth shall mourn. And they shall see the Son of man coming on the clouds of heaven, with great power and majesty. And he shall send out his Angels with a trumpet and a great voice. And they shall gather together his elect from the four winds, from the heights of the heavens, even to their furthest limits. (Matt 24:30-31)
Hail Mary...

Heaven and earth shall pass away, but my words shall not pass away. (Matt 24:35)
Hail Mary...

But about that day and hour no one knows, neither the angels of heaven, nor the Son, but only the Father. (Matt 24:36)
Hail Mary...

The King shall say to those who will be on his right: 'Come, you blessed of my Father. Possess the kingdom prepared for you from the foundation of the world. For I was hungry, and you gave me to eat; I was thirsty, and you gave me to drink; I was a stranger, and you took me in; naked, and you covered me; sick, and you visited me; I was in prison, and you came to me.' (Matt 25:34-36)
Hail Mary...

Amen I say to you, whenever you did this for one of these, the least of my brothers, you did it for me. (Matt 25:40)
Hail Mary...

Taking the chalice, he gave thanks. And he gave it to them, saying: "Drink from this, all of you. For this is my blood of the new covenant, which shall be shed for many as a remission of sins. (Matt 26:27-28)
Hail Mary...

Stay awake and pray, so that you may not enter into temptation. Indeed, the spirit is willing, but the flesh is weak. (Matt 26:41)
Hail Mary...

Behold, I am with you always, even to the end of the age. (Matt 28:20)
Hail Mary...

Glory Be…

Decade 5

Our Father…

The time has been fulfilled and the kingdom of God has drawn near. Repent and believe in the Gospel. (Mrk 1:15)
Hail Mary...

They were all so amazed that they inquired among themselves, saying: "What is this? And what is this new doctrine? For with authority he commands even the unclean spirits, and they obey him." (Mrk 1:27)
Hail Mary...

He acted so that the twelve would be with him, and so that he might send them out to preach. And he gave them authority to cure infirmities, and to cast out demons. (Mrk 3:14-15)
Hail Mary...

Pay attention to what you hear; the measure you give will be the measure you get, and still more will be given you. (Mrk 4:24)
Hail Mary...

For whoever has, to him it shall be given more. And whoever has not, from him even what he has shall be taken away. (Mrk 4:25)
Hail Mary...

Rising up, he rebuked the wind, and he said to the sea: "Silence. Be stilled." And the wind ceased. And a great tranquility occurred. And he said to them: "Why are you afraid? Do you still lack faith?" And they were struck with a great fear. And they said to one another, "Who is this, that both wind and sea obey him?" (Mrk 4:39-40)
Hail Mary...

Go to your own people, in your own house, and announce to them how great are the things that the Lord has done for you, and how he has taken pity on you. (Mrk 5:19)
Hail Mary...

He called the twelve. And he began to send them out in twos, and he gave them authority over unclean spirits. (Mrk 6:7)
Hail Mary...

Jesus, going out, saw a great multitude. And he took pity on them, because they were like sheep without a shepherd, and he began to teach them many things. (Mrk 6:34)
Hail Mary...

In whichever place he entered, in towns or villages or cities, they placed the infirm in the main streets, and they pleaded with him that they might touch even the hem of his garment. And as many as touched him were made healthy. (Mrk 6:56)
Hail Mary...

Glory Be…

Day 19

Decade 1

Our Father…

Whoever will have chosen to save his life, will lose it. But whoever will have lost his life, for my sake and for the Gospel, shall save it. (Mrk 8:35)
Hail Mary...

If you are able! -all things are possible to one who believes. (Mrk 9:23)
Hail Mary...

Whoever, in my name, will give you a cup of water to drink, because you bear the name of Christ: Amen I say to you, he shall not lose his reward. (Mrk 9:41)
Hail Mary...

Allow the little ones to come to me, and do not prohibit them. For it is to such as these that the kingdom of God belongs. Amen I say to you, whoever will not accept the kingdom of God like a little child, will not enter into it. (Mrk 10:14-15)
Hail Mary...

Jesus, gazing at him, loved him, and he said to him: "One thing is lacking to you. Go, sell whatever you have, and give to the poor, and then you will have treasure in heaven. And come, follow me." (Mrk 10:21)
Hail Mary...

Amen I say to you, There is no one who has left behind house, or brothers, or sisters, or father, or mother, or children, or land, for my sake and for the Gospel, who will not receive one hundred times as much, now in this time: houses, and brothers, and sisters, and mothers, and children, and land, with persecutions, and in the future age eternal life. (Mrk 10:29-30)
Hail Mary...

Whoever would become greater shall be your servant; and whoever will be first among you shall be the slave of all. For the Son of Man came not to be served but to serve, and to give his life a ransom for many. (Mrk 10:43-45)
Hail Mary...

Amen I say to you, that whoever will say to this mountain, 'Be taken up and cast into the sea,' and who will not have doubted in his heart, but will have

believed that what he says will come to pass, it shall be done for him. (Mrk 11:23)
Hail Mary...

All things whatever you ask for when praying, believe that you have received them, and they will be yours. (Mrk 11:24)
Hail Mary...

When you stand to pray, if you hold anything against anyone, forgive them, so that your Father, who is in heaven, may also forgive you your sins. But if you will not forgive, neither will your Father, who is in heaven, forgive you your sins. (Mrk 11:25-26)
Hail Mary...

Glory Be...

Decade 2

Our Father...

Go forth to the whole world and preach the Gospel to the whole creation. Whoever will have believed and been baptized will be saved. Yet truly, whoever will not have believed will be condemned. (Mrk 16:15-16)
Hail Mary...

These signs will accompany those who believe. In my name, they shall cast out demons. They will speak in new languages. They will take up serpents, and, if they drink anything deadly, it will not harm them. They shall lay their hands upon the sick, and they will be well. (Mrk 16:17-18)
Hail Mary...

They went forth, and preached the good news everywhere, the Lord worked with them, and confirmed the word with signs that accompanied it. (Mrk 16:20)
Hail Mary...

He will be great, and he will be called the Son of the Most High, and the Lord God will give him the throne of David his father. And he will reign in the house of Jacob for eternity. And his kingdom shall have no end.(Luk 1:32-33)
Hail Mary...

Nothing will be impossible with God. (Luk 1:37)
Hail Mary...

For he has looked with favor on the humility of his handmaid. For behold, from this time, all generations shall call me blessed. For the mighty one has done great things for me, and holy is his name. (Luk 1:47-48)
Hail Mary...

His mercy is from generation to generation for those who fear him. (Luk 1:50)
Hail Mary...

He has accomplished powerful deeds with his arm. He has scattered the proud in the intentions of their heart. He has deposed the powerful from their seat, and he has exalted the humble. (Luk 1:51-52)
Hail Mary...

He has filled the hungry with good things, and the rich he has sent away empty. (Luk 1:53)
Hail Mary...

Blessed is the Lord God of Israel. For he has looked with favor and has brought the redemption of his people. And he has raised up a mighty savior for us, in the house of David his servant (Luk 1:68-69)
Hail Mary...

Glory Be…

Decade 3

Our Father…

John responded by saying to everyone: "Indeed, I baptize you with water. But there will arrive one stronger than me, the thongs of whose sandals I am not worthy to loosen. He will baptize you in the Holy Spirit, and with fire." (Luk 3:16)
Hail Mary...

The Spirit of the Lord is upon me; because of this, he has anointed me. He has sent me to bring good news to the poor, to heal the contrite of heart, to proclaim release to the captives and sight to the blind, to let the oppressed go free, to preach the acceptable year of the Lord. (Luk 4:18-19)
Hail Mary...

Fear fell over them all. And they discussed this among themselves, saying: "What is this word? For with authority and power he commands the unclean spirits, and they depart." (Luk 4:36)
Hail Mary...

When the sun had set, all those who had anyone afflicted with various diseases brought them to him. Then, laying his hands on each one of them, he cured them. (Luk 4:40)
Hail Mary...

It is not those who are well who need a physician, but those who are sick. I have not come to call the righteous, but sinners to repentance. (Luk 5:31-32)
Hail Mary...

The entire crowd was trying to touch him, because power went out from him and healed all. (Luk 6:19)
Hail Mary...

Blessed are you poor, for yours is the kingdom of God. Blessed are you who are hungry now, for you shall be satisfied. Blessed are you who are weeping now, for you shall laugh. (Luk 6:20-21)
Hail Mary...

As you would want others to do to you, do to them also the same. (Luk 6:31)
Hail Mary...

Love your enemies. Do good, and lend, expecting nothing in return. And then your reward will be great, and you will be children of the Most High God, for he is kind to the ungrateful and to the wicked. (Luk 6:35)
Hail Mary...

Do not judge, and you will not be judged. Do not condemn, and you will not be condemned. Forgive, and you will be forgiven. (Luk 6:37)
Hail Mary...

Glory Be…

Decade 4

Our Father…

Give, and it will be given to you: a good measure, pressed down and shaken together and overflowing, will be placed upon your lap. Certainly, the measure you give, will be the measure that you get back. (Luk 6:38)
Hail Mary...

Calling together the twelve Apostles, he gave them power and authority over all demons and to cure diseases. And he sent them to preach the kingdom of God and to heal the sick. (Luk 9:1)
Hail Mary...

Whoever listens to you, listens to me. And whoever rejects you, rejects me. And whoever rejects me, rejects him who sent me. (Luk 10:16)
Hail Mary...

Behold, I have given you authority to tread upon snakes and scorpions, and upon all the powers of the enemy, and nothing will hurt you. (Luk 10:19)
Hail Mary...

I thank you, Father, Lord of heaven and earth, because you have hidden these things from the wise and the learned, and have revealed them to little ones. (Luk 10:21)
Hail Mary...

Ask, and it shall be given to you. Seek, and you shall find. Knock, and it shall be opened to you. For everyone who asks, receives. And whoever seeks, finds. And whoever knocks, it shall be opened to him. (Luk 11:9-10)
Hail Mary...

Therefore, if you, being evil, know how to give good gifts to your children, how much more will your Father give, from heaven, the Holy Spirit to those who ask him? (Luk 11:13)
Hail Mary...

Do not be fearful of those who kill the body, and afterwards can do no more. But I will reveal to you whom you should fear. Fear him who, after he will have killed, has the power to cast into Hell. So I say to you: Fear him. (Luk 12:4-5)
Hail Mary...

Even the very hairs of your head have all been numbered. Therefore, do not be afraid. You are worth more than many sparrows. (Luk 12:7)
Hail Mary...

Do not choose to be anxious about your life, as to what you may eat, nor about your body, as to what you will wear. Life is more than food, and the body is more than clothing. (Luk 12:22-23)
Hail Mary...

Glory Be…

Decade 5
Our Father…

Can any of you by worrying add a single hour to your span of life? Therefore, if you are not capable, in what is so little, why do you worry about the rest? (Luk 12:25-26)
Hail Mary...

Do not keep striving for what you will eat, or what you will drink, and do not keep worrying. For all these things are sought by the nations of the world, and your Father knows that you have need of these things. Instead, seek first the kingdom of God and all these things shall be added to you. (Luk 12:29-31)
Hail Mary...

Sell what you possess and give alms. Make for yourselves purses that will not wear out, a treasure that will not fall short, in heaven, where no thief approaches, and no moth destroys. For where your treasure is, there will your heart be also. (Luk 12:33-34)
Hail Mary...

Strive to enter through the narrow gate. For many, I tell you, will seek to enter and not be able. (Luk 13:24)
Hail Mary...

Everyone who exalts himself shall be humbled, and whoever humbles himself shall be exalted. (Luk 14:11)
Hail Mary...

When you prepare a feast, call the poor, the disabled, the lame, and the blind. And you will be blessed because they do not have a way to repay you. So then, your recompense will be in the resurrection of the righteous. (Luk 14:13-14)
Hail Mary...

If anyone comes to me, and does not hate his father and mother, wife and children, brothers and sisters, and yes, even his own life, he is not able to be my disciple. (Luk 14:26)
Hail Mary...

I say to you, that there will be so much more joy in heaven over one sinner repenting, than over the ninety-nine righteous, who do not need to repent. (Luk 15:7)
Hail Mary...

The son said to him: 'Father, I have sinned against heaven and before you. Now I am not worthy to be called your son.' But the father said to his servants: 'Quickly! Bring out the best robe and clothe him with it. And put a ring on his hand and shoes on his feet. And bring the fatted calf here and kill it. And let us eat and hold a feast. For this son of mine was dead, and has revived; he was lost, and is found.' And they began to feast. (Luk 15:21-24)
Hail Mary...

Whoever is faithful in what is little, is also faithful in much. And whoever is dishonest in what is little, is also dishonest in what is much. (Luk 16:10)
Hail Mary...

Glory Be...

Day 20

Decade 1

Our Father…

If you have faith like a grain of mustard seed, you may say to this mulberry tree, 'Be uprooted, and be planted into the sea.' And it would obey you. (Luk 17:6)

Hail Mary...

The Son of man has come to seek and to save the lost. (Luk 19:10)

Hail Mary...

They will see the Son of man coming on a cloud, with great power and majesty. But when these things begin to happen, lift up your heads and look around you, because your redemption draws near. (Luk 21:28)

Hail Mary...

He said to them: "How foolish and reluctant in heart you are, to believe everything that has been spoken by the Prophets! Was not the Messiah required to suffer these things, and so enter into his glory?" And beginning from Moses and all the Prophets, he interpreted for them, in all the Scriptures, the things that were about him. (Luk 24:25-27)

Hail Mary...

I am sending the Promise of my Father upon you. But you must stay in the city, until such time as you are clothed with power from on high. (Luk 24:49)

Hail Mary...

In the beginning was the Word, and the Word was with God, and the Word was God. (Jn 1:1)

Hail Mary...

Whoever did accept him, those who believed in his name, he gave them the power to become children of God. These are born, not of blood, nor of the will of flesh, nor of the will of man, but of God. (Jn 1:12-13)

Hail Mary...

The Word became flesh, and he lived among us, and we saw his glory, glory like that of an only-begotten Son from the Father, full of grace and truth. (Jn 1:14)

Hail Mary...

On the next day, John saw Jesus coming toward him, and so he said: "Behold, the Lamb of God. Behold, he who takes away the sin of the world." (Jn 1:29)
Hail Mary...

Amen, amen, I say to you, unless one has been born from above, he is not able to see the kingdom of God. (Jn 3:3)
Hail Mary...

Glory Be...

Decade 2

Our Father...

Amen, amen, I say to you, unless one has been born by water and Spirit, he is not able to enter into the kingdom of God. (Jn 3:5)
Hail Mary...

God so loved the world that he gave his only-begotten Son, so that all who believe in him may not perish, but may have eternal life. (Jn 3:16)
Hail Mary...

For God did not send his Son into the world, in order to judge the world, but in order that the world may be saved through him. (Jn 3:17)
Hail Mary...

Whoever believes in him is not judged. But whoever does not believe is already judged, because he does not believe in the name of the only-begotten Son of God. (Jn 3:18)
Hail Mary...

He whom God has sent speaks the words of God. for he gives the Spirit without measure. (Jn 3:34)
Hail Mary...

Whoever believes in the Son has eternal life, but whoever disobeys the Son will not see life, for God's wrath remains on them. (Jn 3:36)
Hail Mary...

If you knew the gift of God, and who it is who is saying to you, 'Give me to drink,' perhaps you would have made a request of him, and he would have given you living water. (Jn 4:10)
Hail Mary...

All who drink from this water will thirst again. But whoever shall drink from the water that I will give to him will not thirst for eternity. Instead, the water that I will give to him will become in him a fountain of water, springing up into eternal life. (Jn 4:13-14)
Hail Mary...

God is Spirit. And so, those who worship him must worship in spirit and in truth. (Jn 4:24)
Hail Mary...

Afterwards, Jesus found him in the temple, and he said to him: "Behold, you have been healed. Do not choose to sin further, otherwise something worse may happen to you." (Jn 5:14)
Hail Mary...

Glory Be…

Decade 3

Our Father…

Just as the Father raises the dead and gives life, so also does the Son give life to whomever he wills. (Jn 5:21)
Hail Mary...

I say to you, that whoever hears my word, and believes in him who sent me, has eternal life, and he does not go into judgment, but instead he crosses from death into life. (Jn 5:24)
Hail Mary...

The hour is coming, and it is now, when the dead shall hear the voice of the Son of God; and those who hear it shall live. (Jn 5:25)
Hail Mary...

Do not be amazed at this. For the hour is coming in which all who are in the grave shall hear the voice of the Son of God. And those who have done good shall go forth to the resurrection of life. Yet truly, those who have done evil shall go to the resurrection of condemnation. (Jn 5:28-29)
Hail Mary...

You study the Scriptures for you think that in them you have eternal life. And it is they that offer testimony about me. (Jn 5:39)
Hail Mary...

Do not work for the food that perishes, but for that which endures to eternal life, which the Son of man will give to you. (Jn 6:27)
Hail Mary...

Amen, amen, I say to you, Moses did not give you bread from heaven, but my Father gives you the true bread from heaven. (Jn 6:32)
Hail Mary...

The bread of God is he who descends from heaven and gives life to the world. (Jn 6:33)

Hail Mary...

I am the bread of life. Whoever comes to me shall not hunger, and whoever believes in me shall never thirst. (Jn 6:35)
Hail Mary...

All that the Father gives to me shall come to me. And whoever comes to me, I will not drive away. (Jn 6:37)
Hail Mary...

Glory Be...

Decade 4

Our Father...

I descended from heaven, not to do my own will, but the will of him who sent me. Yet this is the will of the Father who sent me: that I should lose nothing out of all that he has given to me, but that I should raise them up on the last day. (Jn 6:38-39)
Hail Mary...

This is the will of my Father who sent me: that everyone who sees the Son and believes in him may have eternal life, and I will raise him up on the last day. (Jn 6:40)
Hail Mary...

No one is able to come to me, unless the Father, who has sent me, has drawn him. And I will raise him up on the last day. (Jn 6:44)
Hail Mary...

Amen, amen, I say to you, whoever believes in me has eternal life. (Jn 6:47)
Hail Mary...

Your ancestors ate manna in the desert, and they died. This is the bread which descends from heaven, so that if anyone will eat from it, he may not die. (Jn 6:49-50)
Hail Mary...

I am the living bread that descended from heaven. If anyone eats from this bread, he shall live forever. (Jn 6:51)
Hail Mary...

Amen, amen, I say to you, unless you eat the flesh of the Son of man and drink his blood, you will not have life in you. (Jn 6:53)
Hail Mary...

Whoever eats my flesh and drinks my blood has eternal life, and I will raise him up on the last day. (Jn 6:54)

Hail Mary...

Whoever eats my flesh and drinks my blood abides in me, and I in him. (Jn 6:57)
Hail Mary...

This is the bread that descends from heaven. It is not like the manna that your fathers ate, for they died. Whoever eats this bread shall live forever. (Jn 6:58)
Hail Mary...

Glory Be...

Decade 5

Our Father...

It is the Spirit who gives life. The flesh is useless. The words that I have spoken to you are spirit and life. (Jn 6:63)
Hail Mary...

Then Simon Peter answered him: "Lord, to whom shall we go? You have the words of eternal life. And we have believed, and we recognize that you are the Holy One of God." (Jn 6:68-69)
Hail Mary...

If anyone thirsts, let him come to me and drink: whoever believes in me, just as Scripture says, 'Out of the believer's heart shall flow rivers of living water.' Now he said this about the Spirit, which those who believe in him would soon be receiving. (Jn 7:37-39)
Hail Mary...

I am the light of the world. Whoever follows me does not walk in darkness, but shall have the light of life. (Jn 8:12)
Hail Mary...

He who sent me is with me, and he has not abandoned me alone. For I always do what is pleasing to him. (Jn 8:29)
Hail Mary...

If you will abide in my word, you will truly be my disciples. And you will know the truth, and the truth will set you free. (Jn 8:31-32)
Hail Mary...

If the Son has set you free, then you will truly be free. (Jn 8:36)
Hail Mary...

If anyone will have kept my word, he will not see death for eternity. (Jn 8:51)
Hail Mary...

He who enters through the door is the shepherd of the sheep. The sheep hear his voice, and he calls his own sheep by name, and he leads them out. And when he has sent out his sheep, he goes before them, and the sheep follow him, because they know his voice. (Jn 10:2-4)
Hail Mary...

I am the gate. If anyone has entered through me, he will be saved. And he will come in and go out, and he will find pasture. (Jn 10:9)
Hail Mary...

Glory Be…

Day 21

Decade 1

Our Father…

The thief comes, only so that he may steal and kill and destroy. I have come so that they may have life, and have it more abundantly. (Jn 10:10)
Hail Mary...

I am the good Shepherd. The good Shepherd gives his life for his sheep. (Jn 10:11)
Hail Mary...

I am the good Shepherd, and I know my own, and my own know me. (Jn 10:14)
Hail Mary...

My sheep hear my voice. And I know them, and they follow me. And I give them eternal life, and they will never perish. And no one will seize them from my hand. (Jn 10:27-28)
Hail Mary...

This sickness is not unto death, but for the glory of God, so that the Son of God may be glorified by it. (Jn 11:4)
Hail Mary...

I am the Resurrection and the Life. Whoever believes in me, even though he has died, he shall live. (Jn 11:25)
Hail Mary...

Everyone who lives and believes in me will never die. (Jn 11:26)
Hail Mary...

Father, I thank you that you have heard me. And I know that you hear me always: (Jn 11:41-42)
Hail Mary...

Whoever loves his life, will lose it. And whoever hates his life in this world, preserves it unto eternal life. (Jn 12:24-25)
Hail Mary...

If anyone serves me, let him follow me. And where I am, there too my minister shall be. If anyone has served me, my Father will honor him. (Jn 12:26)
Hail Mary...

Glory Be…

Decade 2

Our Father…

I have come as a light to the world, so that all who believe in me might not remain in darkness. (Jn 12:46)
Hail Mary...

I am not speaking on my own, but from the Father who sent me. He gave a commandment to me as to what I should say and how I should speak. And I know that his commandment is eternal life. The things that I speak, therefore, I speak just as the Father has told me. (Jn 12:49-50)
Hail Mary...

Jesus knew that the hour was approaching when he would pass from this world to the Father. And since he had always loved his own who were in the world, he loved them unto the end. (Jn 13:1)
Hail Mary...

If I, your Lord and Teacher, have washed your feet, you also ought to wash the feet of one another. For I have given you an example, so that just as I have done for you, so also should you do. (Jn 13:14-15)
Hail Mary...

Amen, amen, I say to you, whoever receives anyone whom I send, receives me. And whoever receives me, receives him who sent me. (Jn 13:20)
Hail Mary...

I give you a new commandment: Love one another. Just as I have loved you, so also must you love one another. By this, all shall recognize that you are my disciples: if you will have love for one another. (Jn 13:34-35)
Hail Mary...

Do not let your hearts be troubled. Believe in God. Believe in me also. (Jn 14:1)
Hail Mary...

In my Father's house, there are many dwelling places. If there were not so, would I have told you that I go to prepare a place for you. And if I go and

prepare a place for you, I will return again, and then I will take you to myself, so that where I am, you also may be. (Jn 14:2-3)
Hail Mary...

I am the Way, and the Truth, and the Life. No one comes to the Father, except through me. (Jn 14:6)
Hail Mary...

Whoever believes in me shall also do the works that I do. And, in fact, will do greater things than these, for I go to the Father. (Jn 14:12)
Hail Mary...

Glory Be…

Decade 3

Our Father…

Whatever you shall ask the Father in my name, that I will do, so that the Father may be glorified in the Son. If you shall ask anything of me in my name, that I will do. (Jn 14:13-14)
Hail Mary...

If you love me, keep my commandments. (Jn 14:15)
Hail Mary...

I will ask the Father, and he will give another Advocate to you, so that he may abide with you for eternity. (Jn 14:16)
Hail Mary...

The Spirit of Truth, whom the world cannot receive, because it neither sees him nor knows him. But you shall know him. For he will remain with you, and he will be in you. (Jn 14:17)
Hail Mary...

I will not leave you orphans. I will return to you. Yet a little while and the world will not see me any longer. But you will see me. Because I live, you also will live. (Jn 14:18)
Hail Mary...

Whoever holds to my commandments and keeps them: it is he who loves me. And whoever loves me shall be loved by my Father. And I will love him, and I will manifest myself to him. (Jn 14:21)
Hail Mary...

If anyone loves me, he shall keep my word. And my Father will love him, and we will come to him, and we will make our dwelling place with him. (Jn 14:23)
Hail Mary...

The Advocate, the Holy Spirit, whom the Father will send in my name, will teach you all things and will remind you everything that I have said to you. (Jn 14:26)
Hail Mary...

Peace I leave for you; my Peace I give to you. Not in the way that the world gives, do I give to you. Do not let your heart be troubled, and let it not fear. (Jn 14:27)
Hail Mary...

Every branch in me that does not bear fruit, he will take away. And each one that does bear fruit, he will cleanse, so that it may bring forth more fruit. (Jn 15:2)
Hail Mary...

Glory Be…

Decade 4
Our Father…

You are clean now, because of the word that I have spoken to you. (Jn 15:3)
Hail Mary...

I am the vine; you are the branches. Whoever abides in me, and I in him, bears much fruit. For without me, you can do nothing. (Jn 15:5)
Hail Mary...

If you abide in me, and my words abide in you, then you may ask for whatever you wish, and it will be done for you. (Jn 15:7)
Hail Mary...

In this, my Father is glorified: that you should bear much fruit and become my disciples. (Jn 15:8)
Hail Mary...

As the Father has loved me, so I have loved you. Abide in my love. If you keep my commandments, you shall abide in my love, just as I also have kept my Father's commandments and I abide in his love. (Jn 15:9-10)
Hail Mary...

No one has a greater love than this: that he lay down his life for his friends. You are my friends, if you do what I instruct you. (Jn 15:13-14)
Hail Mary...

I will no longer call you servants, for the servant does not know what his Lord is doing. But I have called you friends, because everything whatsoever that I have heard from my Father, I have made known to you. (Jn 15:15)
Hail Mary...

You have not chosen me, but I have chosen you. And I have appointed you, so that you may go forth and bear fruit, fruit that will last. Then whatever you have asked of the Father in my name, he will give to you. (Jn 15:16)
Hail Mary...

If the world hates you, know that it has hated me before you. If you had been of the world, the world would love you as its own. Yet truly, you are not of the world, but I have chosen you out of the world; because of this, the world hates you. (Jn 15:18-19)
Hail Mary...

Nevertheless I tell you the truth: it is to your advantage that I go away, for if I do not go away, the Advocate will not come to you; but if I go, I will send him to you. (Jn 16:7)
Hail Mary...

Glory Be…

Decade 5
Our Father…

When he will come, he will prove the world wrong about sin, and of righteousness, and of judgment. (Jn 16:8)
Hail Mary...

When the Spirit of truth comes, he will teach the whole truth to you. For he will not be speaking from himself. Instead, whatever he will hear, he will speak. And he will announce to you the things that are to come. (Jn 16:13)
Hail Mary...

He shall glorify me. For he will receive from what is mine, and he will announce it to you. All things whatsoever that the Father has are mine. For this reason, I said that he will receive from what is mine and that he will announce it to you. (Jn 16:14-15)
Hail Mary...

Amen, amen, I say to you, that you shall mourn and weep, but the world will rejoice. And you shall be greatly saddened, yet your sorrow shall be turned into joy. (Jn 16:20)
Hail Mary...

Therefore, you also, indeed, have sorrow now. But I will see you again, and your heart shall rejoice. And no one will take away your joy from you. (Jn 16:22)
Hail Mary...

Amen, amen, I say to you, if you ask the Father for anything in my name, he will give it to you. Until now, you have not requested anything in my name. Ask, and you shall receive, so that your joy may be full. (Jn 16:23-24)
Hail Mary...

These things I have spoken to you, so that you may have peace in me. In the world, you will face persecutions. But take courage: I have conquered the world. (Jn 16:33)
Hail Mary...

This is eternal life: that they may know you, the only true God, and Jesus Christ, whom you have sent. (Jn 17:3)
Hail Mary...

Sanctify them in truth. Your word is truth. (Jn 17:17)
Hail Mary...

I am not praying for them only, but also for those who through their word shall believe in me. So may they all be one. Just as you, Father, are in me, and I am in you, so also may they be one in us: so that the world may believe that you have sent me. (Jn 17:21)
Hail Mary...

Glory Be...

Day 22

Decade 1

Our Father…

I in them and you in me so may they become completely one. And may the world know that you have sent me and that you have loved them, just as you have also loved me. (Jn 17:23)

Hail Mary….

I have made known your name to them, and I will make it known, so that the love in which you have loved me may be in them, and so that I may be in them. (Jn 17:26)

Hail Mary...

He said to them again: "Peace to you. As the Father has sent me, so I send you." When he had said this, he breathed on them. And he said to them: "Receive the Holy Spirit. Those whose sins you shall forgive, they are forgiven them, and those whose sins you retain, they are retained." (Jn 20:21-23)

Hail Mary...

Blessed are those who have not seen and yet have believed. (Jn 20:29)

Hail Mary...

And dining with them, he instructed them that they should not depart from Jerusalem, but that they should wait for the Promise of the Father, "about which you have heard," he said, "from my own mouth. For John, indeed, baptized with water, but you shall be baptized with the Holy Spirit, not many days from now." (Acts 1:4-5)

Hail Mary...

You will receive power when the Holy Spirit has come over you, and you will be my witnesses in Jerusalem, and in all Judea and Samaria, and even to the ends of the earth. (Acts 1:8)

Hail Mary..

They said: "Men of Galilee, why do you stand here looking up toward heaven? This Jesus, who has been taken up from you into heaven, shall return in just the same way that you have seen him going up to heaven." (Acts 1:11)

Hail Mary...

They were all filled with the Holy Spirit. And they began to speak in various languages, just as the Holy Spirit gave them ability. (Acts 2:4)
Hail Mary...

In the last days, says the Lord, I will pour out my Spirit, upon all flesh. And your sons and your daughters shall prophesy. And your youths shall see visions, and your elders shall dream dreams. (Acts 2:17)
Hail Mary...

The sun shall be turned into darkness and the moon into blood, before the great and glorious day of the Lord arrives. And this shall be: whoever shall invoke the name of the Lord will be saved. (Acts 2:20-21)
Hail Mary...

Glory Be…

Decade 2

Our Father…

I saw the Lord always before me, for he is at my right hand, so that I may not be moved. Because of this, my heart has rejoiced, and my tongue has exulted. Moreover, my flesh will also rest in hope. (Acts 2:25-26)
Hail Mary...

Therefore, being exalted to the right hand of God, and having received from the Father the Promise of the Holy Spirit, he poured this out, just as you now see and hear. (Acts 2:33)
Hail Mary...

Repent and be baptized, each one of you, in the name of Jesus Christ, for the remission of your sins. And you shall receive the gift of the Holy Spirit. (Acts 2:38)
Hail Mary...

Day by day, as they spent much time together in the temple, they broke bread at home and ate their food with glad and generous hearts, praising God and having the goodwill of all the people. And day by day the Lord added to their number those who were being saved. (Acts 2:46-47)
Hail Mary...

Through faith in his name has made this man strong, whom you see and know: and the faith which is through Jesus has given him this perfect health in the presence of you all. (Acts 3:16)
Hail Mary...

Repent and be converted, so that your sins may be wiped away. (Acts 3:19)

Hail Mary...

When the time of refreshing will have arrived from the presence of the Lord, he will send the One who was foretold to you, Jesus Christ, whom heaven certainly must take up, until the time of the restoration of all things, which God has spoken of by the mouth of his holy prophets, from ages past. (Acts 3:20-21)
Hail Mary...

Let it be known to all of you and to all of the people of Israel, that in the name of our Lord Jesus Christ the Nazarene, whom you crucified, whom God has raised from the dead, by him, this man stands before you, healthy. (Acts 4:10)
Hail Mary...

Jesus is the one of whom the scripture says, 'The stone that you the builders rejected turned out to be the cornerstone.' There is no salvation in any other. For there is no other name under heaven given to men, by which we must be saved. (Acts 4:11-12)
Hail Mary...

And now, O Lord, look upon their threats, and grant to your servants that they may speak your word with all confidence, by extending your hand in cures and signs and miracles, to be done through the name of your holy Son, Jesus. (Acts 4:29-30)
Hail Mary...

Glory Be...

Decade 3

Our Father...

When they had prayed, the place in which they were gathered was moved. And they were all filled with the Holy Spirit. And they were speaking the Word of God with confidence. (Acts 4:31)
Hail Mary...

With great power, the Apostles were rendering testimony to the Resurrection of Jesus Christ our Lord. And great grace was in them all. (Acts 4:33)
Hail Mary...

Through the hands of the Apostles many signs and wonders were accomplished among the people. (Acts 5:12)
Hail Mary...

A multitude also hurried to Jerusalem from the neighboring cities, carrying the sick and those troubled by unclean spirits, and they were all healed. (Acts 5:16)
Hail Mary...

We are witnesses of these things, with the Holy Spirit, whom God has given to all who are obedient to him. (Acts 5:32)
Hail Mary...

The crowd was listening intently and with one accord to those things which were being said by Philip, and they were watching the signs which he was accomplishing. For many of them had unclean spirits, and, crying out with a loud voice, these departed from them. And many of the paralytics and the lame were cured. (Acts 8:6-8)
Hail Mary...

God is not a respecter of persons. But within every nation, whoever fears him and does what is right is acceptable to him. (Acts 10:34-35)
Hail Mary...

God sent the Word to the people of Israel, announcing the peace through Jesus Christ, for he is the Lord of all. (Acts 10:36)
Hail Mary...

Jesus of Nazareth, whom God anointed with the Holy Spirit and with power, traveled around doing good and healing all those oppressed by the devil. For God was with him. (Acts 10:38)
Hail Mary...

To him all the Prophets offer testimony that through his name all who believe in him receive forgiveness of sins. (Acts 10:43)
Hail Mary...

Glory Be…

Decade 4
Our Father…

While Peter was still speaking these words, the Holy Spirit fell over all of those who were listening to the Word. (Acts 10:44)
Hail Mary...

By this Jesus everyone who believes is set free from all those sins from which you could not be freed by the law of Moses. (Acts 13:39)
Hail Mary...

It is through many persecutions that we must enter into the kingdom of God. (Acts 14:22)
Hail Mary...

In the middle of the night, Paul and Silas were praying and praising God. And those who were also in custody were listening to them. Yet truly, there was a sudden earthquake, so great that the foundations of the prison were moved. And immediately all the doors were opened, and the chains of everyone were released. (Acts 16:25-26)
Hail Mary...

Believe in the Lord Jesus, and then you will be saved, you and your household. (Acts 16:31)
Hail Mary...

The God who made the world and all that is in it, the One who is the Lord of heaven and earth, who does not live in temples made with hands. Neither is he served by the hands of men, as though he needed anything, since it is he who gives to all things life and breath and all else. (Acts 17:24-25)
Hail Mary...

God, having looked down to see the ignorance of these times, has now announced to men that everyone everywhere should do penance. (Acts 17:30)
Hail Mary...

He has appointed a day on which he will judge the world in equity, through the man whom he has appointed, offering faith to all, by raising him from the dead. (Acts 17:31)
Hail Mary...

The Lord said to Paul, through a vision in the night: "Do not be afraid. Instead, speak out and do not be silent. For I am with you. And no one will take hold of you, so as to do you harm." (Acts 18:9-10)
Hail Mary...

When Paul had imposed his hands on them, the Holy Spirit came over them. And they were speaking in tongues and prophesying. (Acts 19:6)
Hail Mary...

Glory Be…

Decade 5
Our Father…

God was accomplishing powerful and uncommon miracles by the hand of Paul, so much so that even when the handkerchiefs or wrappings were brought from his body to the sick, the illnesses withdrew from them and the wicked spirits departed. (Acts 19:11-12)
Hail Mary...

Rise up and stand on your feet. For I appeared to you for this reason: so that I may establish you as a minister and a witness concerning the things that you have seen, and concerning the things that I will show to you: rescuing you from the people and the nations to which I am now sending you, in order to open their eyes, so that they may be converted from darkness to light, and from the power of Satan to God, so that they may receive the remission of sins and a place among the saints, by faith in me. (Acts 26:16-18)
Hail Mary...

It happened that the father of Publius lay ill with a fever and with dysentery. Paul visited him, and when he had prayed and had laid his hands on him, he cured him. When this had been done, all who had diseases on the island approached and were cured. (Acts 28:8-9)
Hail Mary...

I am not ashamed of the Gospel. For it is the power of God unto salvation for all believers, the Jew first, and the Greek. (Rom 1:16)
Hail Mary...

The righteous one will live by faith. (Rom 1:17)
Hail Mary...

He will render to each one according to his works: To those who, in accord with patient good works, seek glory and honor and incorruption, certainly, he will render eternal life. But to those who are contentious and who do not obey the truth, but instead trust in iniquity, he will render wrath and indignation. (Rom 2:6-7)
Hail Mary...

There is no favoritism with God. (Rom 2:11)
Hail Mary...

What if some of them were unfaithful? Shall their unfaithfulness nullify the faithfulness of God? Let it not be so! For God is truthful, although every man is a liar. (Rom 3:3-4)
Hail Mary...

Now, apart from the law, the righteousness of God, to which the law and the prophets have testified, has been made manifest. And the righteousness of

God, through the faith of Jesus Christ, is in all those and over all those who believe in him. (Rom 3:22)
Hail Mary...

We have been justified freely by his grace through the redemption that is in Christ Jesus, whom God has offered as a sacrifice of atonement, through faith in his blood, to reveal his justice for the remission of the former sins. (Rom 3:24-25)
Hail Mary...

Glory Be…

Day 23

Decade 1

Our Father…

Blessed are they whose iniquities have been forgiven and whose sins have been covered. Blessed is the man to whom the Lord has not imputed sin. (Rom 4:7-8)

Hail Mary...

In the Promise of God, he did not waver out of distrust, but instead he was strengthened in faith, giving glory to God, knowing most fully that whatever God has promised, he is also able to accomplish. (Rom 4:20-21)

Hail Mary...

Therefore, having been justified by faith, we are at peace with God, through our Lord Jesus Christ. (Rom 5:1)

Hail Mary...

Through Jesus we also have access by faith to this grace, in which we stand firm, and boast in the hope of sharing the glory of God. (Rom 5:2)

Hail Mary...

We even boast in suffering, knowing that suffering leads to endurance, and endurance leads to character, and character leads to hope, and this hope does not disappoint. (Rom 5:3-5)

Hail Mary...

God's love is poured forth in our hearts through the Holy Spirit that has been given to us. (Rom 5:5)

Hail Mary...

God proves his love for us in that, while we were yet sinners, at the proper time, Christ died for us. (Rom 5:8)

Hail Mary...

For if we were reconciled to God through the death of his Son, while we were still enemies, all the more so, having been reconciled, shall we be saved by his life. And not only that, but we also glory in God through our Lord Jesus Christ, through whom we have now received reconciliation. (Rom 5:10-11)

Hail Mary...

If by the one man's offense, death exercised dominion through that one, yet so much more so shall those who receive an abundance of grace and the gift

of righteousness, exercise dominion in life through the one Jesus Christ. (Rom 5:17)
Hail Mary...

Just as through the disobedience of one man, many were established as sinners, so also through the obedience of one man, many will be established as righteous. (Rom 5:19)
Hail Mary...

Glory Be…

Decade 2

Our Father…

Do you not know that those of us who have been baptized in Christ Jesus have been baptized into his death? For through baptism we have been buried with him into death, so that, in the manner that Christ rose from the dead, by the glory of the Father, so may we also walk in the newness of life. (Rom 6:3-4)
Hail Mary...

We know this: that our former selves have been crucified together with him, so that the body which is of sin may be destroyed, and moreover, so that we may no longer serve sin. For he who has died has been justified from sin. (Rom 6:6-7)
Hail Mary...

Sin will not have dominion over you. For you are not under the law, but under grace. (Rom 6:14)
Hail Mary...

Do you not know to whom you are offering yourselves as servants under obedience? You are the servants of whomever you obey: whether of sin, unto death, or of obedience, unto righteousness. (Rom 6:16)
Hail Mary...

Now that you are freed from sin, and having been made servants of God, the fruit you receive is sanctification, and truly the end is eternal life. (Rom 6:22)
Hail Mary...

The wages of sin is death. But the free gift of God is eternal life in Christ Jesus our Lord. (Rom 6:23)
Hail Mary...

We have been released from the law of death, by which we were being held captive, so that are slaves not under the old written law, but in the new life in the spirit. (Rom 7:6)

Hail Mary...

Wretched man that I am, who will free me from this body of death? Thanks to God, by Jesus Christ our Lord! (Rom 7:24-25)
Hail Mary...

Therefore, there is now no condemnation for those who are in Christ Jesus. (Rom 8:1)
Hail Mary...

The law of the Spirit of life in Christ Jesus has freed me from the law of sin and death. (Rom 8:2)
Hail Mary...

Glory Be...

Decade 3

Our Father...

God sent his own Son in the likeness of sinful flesh and because of sin, in order to condemn sin in the flesh, so that the justification of the law might be fulfilled in us. For we are not walking according to the flesh, but according to the spirit. (Rom 8:3-4)
Hail Mary...

Those who are in agreement with the flesh are mindful of the things of the flesh. But those who are in agreement with the spirit are mindful of the things of the spirit. (Rom 8:5)
Hail Mary...

To set the mind on the flesh is death, but to set the mind on the Spirit is life and peace. (Rom 8:6)
Hail Mary...

If Christ is within you, then the body is indeed dead, because of sin, but the spirit truly lives, because of righteousness. (Rom 8:10)
Hail Mary...

If the Spirit of him who raised up Jesus from the dead lives within you, then he who raised up Jesus Christ from the dead will also give life to your mortal bodies, by means of his Spirit living within you. (Rom 8:11)
Hail Mary...

If you live according to the flesh, you will die. But if, by the Spirit, you mortify the deeds of the flesh, you shall live. (Rom 8:13)
Hail Mary...

For all those who are led by the Spirit of God are children of God. (Rom 8:14)

Hail Mary...

You have not received a spirit of slavery to fall back into fear, but you have received the Spirit of adoption, in whom we cry out: "Abba, Father!" For the Spirit himself renders testimony to our spirit that we are children of God. (Rom 8:15-16)
Hail Mary...

I consider that the sufferings of this time are not worthy to be compared with that future glory which shall be revealed in us. (Rom 8:18)
Hail Mary...

We have been saved by hope. But a hope which is seen is not hope. For when a man sees something, why would he hope? But since we hope for what we do not see, we wait for it with patience. (Rom 8:24-25)
Hail Mary...

Glory Be…

Decade 4

Our Father…

The Spirit also helps our weakness. For we do not know how to pray as we ought, but the Spirit himself asks on our behalf with sighs too deep for words. And he who examines hearts knows what the Spirit seeks, because he asks on behalf of the saints in accordance with God. (Rom 8:26-27)
Hail Mary...

We know that all things work together unto good for those who love God, who are called in accordance with his purpose. (Rom 8:28)
Hail Mary...

Those whom he foreknew, he also predestined, in conformity with the image of his Son, so that he might be the Firstborn within a family. And those whom he predestined, he also called. And those whom he called, he also justified. And those whom he justified, he also glorified. (Rom 8:29)
Hail Mary...

What should we say about these things? If God is for us, who is against us? (Rom 8:31)
Hail Mary...

He who did not spare even his own Son, but handed him over for the sake of us all, will he not with him also give us everything else? (Rom 8:32)
Hail Mary...

Christ Jesus who has died, and who has indeed also risen again, is at the right hand of God, who indeed intercedes for us. (Rom 8:34)
Hail Mary...

Who will separate us from the love of Christ? Tribulation? or anguish? or famine? or nakedness? or peril? or persecution? or the sword? In all these things we are more than conquerors, because of him who has loved us. (Rom 8:35, 37)
Hail Mary...

I am certain that neither death, nor life, nor angels, nor principalities, nor Powers, nor the present things, nor the future things, nor strength, nor the heights, nor the depths, nor any other created thing, will be able to separate us from the love of God, which is in Christ Jesus our Lord. (Rom 8:38-39)
Hail Mary...

The end of the law is Christ, so that there may be righteousness for all who believe. (Rom 10:4)
Hail Mary...

For if you confess with your mouth the Lord Jesus, and if you believe in your heart that God has raised him up from the dead, you shall be saved. (Rom 10:9)
Hail Mary...

Glory Be...

Decade 5

Our Father...

For with the heart, we believe and we are justified; and with the mouth, we confess and we are saved. (Rom 10:10)
Hail Mary...

There is no distinction between Jew and Greek. For the same Lord is Lord over all, and is generous to all who call upon him. For all those who have called upon the name of the Lord shall be saved. (Rom 10:12)
Hail Mary...

Everyone who has called upon the name of the Lord shall be saved. (Rom 10:13)
Hail Mary...

Faith comes from what is heard, and what is heard comes through the word of Christ. (Rom 10:17)
Hail Mary...

I beg you, brothers, by the mercy of God, that you offer your bodies as a living sacrifice, holy and pleasing to God, which is your spiritual worship. (Rom 12:1)
Hail Mary...

Do not choose to be conformed to this world, but instead choose to be renewed in the newness of your mind, so that you may discern what is the will of God: what is good, and what is well-pleasing, and what is perfect. (Rom 12:2)
Hail Mary...

Rejoice in hope; be patient in tribulation; persevere in prayer. (Rom 12:12)
Hail Mary...

Do not take revenge, dearest ones. Instead, step aside from wrath. For it is written: "Vengeance is mine. I shall give retribution, says the Lord." (Rom 12:19)
Hail Mary...

You should owe nothing to anyone, except so as to love one another. For whoever loves his neighbor has fulfilled the law. (Rom 13:8)
Hail Mary...

Love does no harm to a neighbor. Therefore, love is the fulfilling of the law. (Rom 13:10)
Hail Mary...

Glory Be…

Day 24

Decade 1

Our Father…

He who observes the day, observes for the Lord. And he who eats, eats for the Lord; for he gives thanks to God. And he who does not eat, does not eat for the Lord, and he gives thanks to God. (Rom 14:6)
Hail Mary...

If we live, we live for the Lord, and if we die, we die for the Lord. Therefore, whether we live or die, we belong to the Lord. (Rom 14:8)
Hail Mary...

Christ died and rose again for this purpose: that he might be the Lord of the living and the dead. (Rom 14:9)
Hail Mary...

The kingdom of God is not food and drink, but righteousness and peace and joy, in the Holy Spirit. (Rom 14:17)
Hail Mary...

Whatever was written, was written to teach us, so that, through patience and the consolation of the Scriptures, we might have hope. (Rom 15:4)
Hail Mary...

May the God of patience and comfort grant you to be of one mind toward one another, in accord with Jesus Christ, so that, together with one mouth, you may glorify the God and Father of our Lord Jesus Christ. (Rom 15:5-6)
Hail Mary...

May the God of hope fill you with every joy and with peace in believing, so that you may abound in hope and in the virtue of the Holy Spirit. (Rom 15:13)
Hail Mary...

The God of peace will quickly crush Satan under your feet. The grace of our Lord Jesus Christ be with you. (Rom 16:20)
Hail Mary...

God is faithful. Through him, you have been called into the fellowship of his Son, Jesus Christ our Lord. (1 Cor 1:9)
Hail Mary...

The message about the Cross is certainly foolishness to those who are perishing. But to us who are being saved, it is the power of God. (1 Cor 1:18)
Hail Mary...

Glory Be…

Decade 2

Our Father…

The eye has not seen, and the ear has not heard, nor has it been conceived by the human heart, what things God has prepared for those who love him. But God has revealed these things to us through his Spirit. For the Spirit searches all things, even the depths of God. (1 Cor 2:9-10)
Hail Mary...

We have not received the spirit of this world, but the Spirit who is of God, so that we may understand the things that have been given to us by God. (1 Cor 2:12)
Hail Mary...

The person who is spiritual can discern everything but is not subject to anyone's judgment. (1 Cor 2:14-15)
Hail Mary...

I planted, Apollo watered, but God provided the growth. And so, neither he who plants, nor he who waters, is anything, but only God, who provides the growth. (1 Cor 3:7)
Hail Mary...

Do you not know that you are the Temple of God, and that the Spirit of God lives within you? But if anyone violates the Temple of God, God will destroy him. For the Temple of God is holy, and you are that Temple. (1 Cor 3:16-17)
Hail Mary...

What do you have that you have not received? But if you have received it, why do you glory, as if you had not received it? (1 Cor 4:7)
Hail Mary...

You have been washed, you have been sanctified, and you have been justified: all in the name of our Lord Jesus Christ and in the Spirit of our God. (1 Cor 6:11)
Hail Mary...

All things are lawful to me, but all things are not beneficial: all things are lawful for me, but I will not be dominated under the power of anything. (1 Cor 6:12)

Hail Mary...

Do you not know that your bodies are the Temple of the Holy Spirit, who is in you, whom you have from God, and that you are not your own? For you have been bought at a great price. Glorify God in your body. (1 Cor 6:19-20)
Hail Mary...

We know that there is only one God, the Father, from whom all things are, and in whom we exist, and one Lord Jesus Christ, through whom all things are, and by whom we live. (1 Cor 8:6)
Hail Mary...

Glory Be…

Decade 3
Our Father…

No temptation has overtaken you such as is not common to everyone: but God is faithful, who will not let you be tested beyond what you are able; but with the temptation he will also make a way to escape, so that you may be able to endure it. (1 Cor 10:13)
Hail Mary...

The cup of blessing that we bless, is it not a communion in the Blood of Christ? And the bread that we break, is it not a sharing in the Body of Christ? (1 Cor 10:16)
Hail Mary...

Through the one bread, we, though many, are one body: all of us who are partakers of the one bread. (1 Cor 10:17)
Hail Mary...

Whether you eat or drink, or whatever else you may do, do everything for the glory of God. (1 Cor 10:31)
Hail Mary...

I have received from the Lord what I have also handed on to you: that the Lord Jesus, on the same night that he was handed over, took bread, and giving thanks, he broke it, and said: "Take and eat. This is my body, which shall be given up for you. Do this in remembrance of me." (1 Cor 11:23-24)
Hail Mary...

Similarly also, the cup, after he had eaten supper, saying: "This cup is the new covenant in my blood. Do this, as often as you drink it, in remembrance of me." (1 Cor 11:25)
Hail Mary...

As often as you eat this bread and drink this cup, you proclaim the death of the Lord, until he returns. (1 Cor 11:26)
Hail Mary...

When we are judged, we are being corrected by the Lord, so that we might not be condemned along with this world. (1 Cor 11:32)
Hail Mary...

No one speaking in the Spirit of God utters a curse against Jesus. And no one is able to say that Jesus is Lord, except in the Holy Spirit. (1 Cor 12:3)
Hail Mary...

The manifestation of the Spirit is given to each one toward what is beneficial. Certainly, to one, through the Spirit, is given words of wisdom; but to another, according to the same Spirit, words of knowledge; to another, in the same Spirit, faith; to another, in the one Spirit, the gift of healing; to another, miraculous works; to another, prophecy; to another, the discernment of spirits; to another, different kinds of tongues; to another, the interpretation of tongues. (1 Cor 12:7-10)
Hail Mary...

Glory Be…

Decade 4

Our Father…

Indeed, in one Spirit, we were all baptized into one body, whether Jews or Gentiles, whether servant or free. And we all drank in the one Spirit. (1 Cor 12:13)
Hail Mary...

If I were to speak in the language of men, or of Angels, but do not have love, I would be like a clanging bell or a crashing cymbal. And if I have prophecy, and learn every mystery, and obtain all knowledge, and possess all faith, so that I could move mountains, yet not have love, then I am nothing. And if I distribute all my goods in order to feed the poor, and if I hand over my body to be burned, yet not have love, it profits me nothing. (1 Cor 13:1-3)
Hail Mary...

Love is patient, love is kind. Love does not envy, does not act wrongly, is not inflated. Love is not ambitious, does not seek for itself, is not provoked to anger. Love does not rejoice over iniquity, but rejoices in truth. Love bears all things, believes all things, hopes all things, endures all things. (1 Cor 13:4-7)
Hail Mary...

Love never fails, But prophecies will come to an end, or tongues, they will cease, or knowledge it will come to an end. (1 Cor 13:8)
Hail Mary...

Now we see through a mirror dimly. But then we shall see face to face. Now I know in part, but then I will know fully, even as I am fully known. (1 Cor 13:12)
Hail Mary...

But for now, these three continue: faith, hope, and love. And the greatest of these is love. (1 Cor 13:13)
Hail Mary...

Now if Christ is preached, that he rose again from the dead, how is it that some among you say that there is no resurrection of the dead? For if there is no resurrection of the dead, then Christ has not risen. And if Christ has not risen, then our preaching is useless, and your faith is also useless. (1 Cor 15:12-14)
Hail Mary...

If for this life only we have hoped in Christ, then we are most to be pitied than all people. (1 Cor 15:19)
Hail Mary...

For certainly, death came through a man. And so, the resurrection of the dead came through a man And just as in Adam all die, so also in Christ all will be brought to life. (1 Cor 15:21-22)
Hail Mary...

Certainly, we shall all rise again, but we shall all be transformed: in a moment, in the twinkling of an eye, at the last trumpet. For the trumpet will sound, and the dead will rise up, incorruptible. And we shall be transformed. Thus, it is necessary for this corruptibility to be clothed with incorruptibility, and for this mortality to be clothed with immortality. (1 Cor 15:51-53)
Hail Mary...

Glory Be…

Decade 5
Our Father…

Be steadfast and unmovable, abounding always in the work of the Lord, knowing that your labor is not useless in the Lord. (1 Cor 15:58)
Hail Mary...

Be vigilant. Stand firm in faith. Be courageous and be strengthened. (1 Cor 16:13)
Hail Mary...

Blessed be the God and Father of our Lord Jesus Christ, the Father of mercies and the God of all consolation. He consoles us in all our tribulation, so that we too may be able to console those who are in any kind of distress, through the consolation by which we also are being consoled by God. (2 Cor 1:3-4)
Hail Mary...

For in him, every one of the promises of God is a "Yes". For this reason it is through him that we say Amen to the glory of God. (2 Cor 1:20)
Hail Mary...

He has sealed us, and he has placed the pledge of the Spirit in our hearts. (2 Cor 1:22)
Hail Mary...

Anyone whom you have forgiven of anything, I also forgive. And then, too, anyone I have forgiven, if I have forgiven anything, it was done in the person of Christ for your sakes, so that we would not be circumvented by Satan. For we are not ignorant of his intentions. (2 Cor 2:10-11)
Hail Mary...

Now the Spirit is Lord. And wherever the Spirit of the Lord is, there is liberty. (2 Cor 3:17)
Hail Mary...

Truly, all of us, as we gaze upon the unveiled glory of the face of the Lord, are transfigured into the same image, from one glory to another. And this is done by the Spirit of the Lord. (2 Cor 3:18)
Hail Mary...

We are afflicted on every side, yet not distressed; we are perplexed, but not in despair; Persecuted, but not forsaken; cast down, but not destroyed; Always carrying in the body the death of our Lord Jesus, so that the life also of Jesus might be made visible in our body. (2 Cor 4:8-10)
Hail Mary...

For we who live are ever handed over unto death for the sake of Jesus, so that the life of Jesus may also be manifested in our mortal flesh. (2 Cor 4:11)
Hail Mary...

Glory Be…

Day 25

Decade 1

Our Father…
Therefore we do not lose heart. Even though our outward man is perishing, yet the inner self is being renewed day by day. (2 Cor 4:16)
Hail Mary...

For though our affliction is, at the present time, temporary and light, it accomplishes in us the weight of a sublime eternal glory, beyond measure. And we are looking at, not the things that are seen, but the things that are unseen. For the things that are seen are temporary, whereas the things that are not seen are eternal. (2 Cor 4:17-18)
Hail Mary...

We know that, when our earthly house of this habitation is dissolved, we have a building of God, a house not made with hands, eternal in heaven. (2 Cor 5:1)
Hail Mary...

We walk by faith, and not by sight. (2 Cor 5:7)
Hail Mary...

We are confident and have a good will to be away from the body and to be at home with the Lord. And therefore we labor, whether at home or away from the body, to please him. (2 Cor 5:8-9)
Hail Mary...

For it is necessary for us to appear before the judgment seat of Christ, so that each one may receive recompense for what has been done in the body, whether it was good or evil. (2 Cor 5:10)
Hail Mary...

Christ died for all, so that even those who live might not now live for themselves, but for him who died for them and who rose again. (2 Cor 5:15)
Hail Mary...

If anyone is a new creation in Christ, what is old has passed away. Behold, all things have been made new. (2 Cor 5:17)
Hail Mary...

All is of God, who has reconciled us to himself through Christ, and who has given us the ministry of reconciliation. For certainly God was in Christ,

reconciling the world to himself, not charging them with their sins. And he has placed in us the ministry of reconciliation. (2 Cor 5:18-19)
Hail Mary...

God made him who did not know sin to be sin for us, so that we might become the righteousness of God in him. (2 Cor 5:21)
Hail Mary...

Glory Be...

Decade 2
Our Father...

You are the temple of the living God, just as God says: "I will dwell with them, and I will walk among them. And I will be their God, and they shall be my people." (2 cor 6:16)
Hail Mary...

Therefore, having these promises, most beloved, let us cleanse ourselves from all defilement of the flesh and of the spirit, perfecting holiness in the fear of God. (2 Cor 7:1)
Hail Mary...

Sorrow that is according to God accomplishes a repentance which leads unto salvation. But the sorrow that is of the world produces death. (2 Cor 7:10)
Hail Mary...

You know the grace of our Lord Jesus Christ, that though he was rich, he became poor for your sakes, so that through his poverty, you might become rich. (2 Cor 8:9)
Hail Mary...

Whoever sows sparingly will also reap sparingly. And whoever sows bountifully shall also reap bountifully: each one giving, just as he has determined in his heart, neither out of sadness, nor out of obligation. For God loves a cheerful giver. (2 Cor 9:6-7)
Hail Mary...

God is able to make every blessing abound in you, so that, always having what you need in all things, you may abound unto every good work. (2 Cor 9:8)
Hail Mary...

He who ministers seed to the sower will offer you bread to eat, and will multiply your seed, and will increase the growth of the fruits of your righteousness. (2 Cor 9:10)
Hail Mary...

For though we walk in the flesh, we do not battle according to the flesh. (2 Cor 10:3)
Hail Mary...

The weapons of our battles are not merely human, but they have divine power to pull down strongholds: tearing down every argument and obstacle that extols itself contrary to the wisdom of God, and we take every thought captive to obey to Christ. (2 Cor 10:4-5)
Hail Mary...

Let the one who boasts, boast in the Lord. For it is not those who commend themselves that are approved, but those whom the Lord commends. (2 Cor 10:17-18)
Hail Mary...

Glory Be…

Decade 3
Our Father…

He said to me: "My grace is sufficient for you. For power is perfected in weakness." And so, willingly shall I glory in my weaknesses, so that the power of Christ may live within me. (2 Cor 12:9)
Hail Mary...

I am content with weaknesses, in reproaches, in difficulties, in persecutions, in distresses, for the sake of Christ. For when I am weak, then I am strong. (2 Cor 12:10)
Hail Mary...

He is not weak with you but is powerful with you. For although he was crucified in weakness, yet he lives by the power of God. And yes, we are weak in him. But we shall live with him by the power of God. (2 Cor 13:3-4)
Hail Mary...

Rejoice, be perfect, be encouraged, have the same mind, live in peace. And so the God of peace and love will be with you. (2 Cor 13:11)
Hail Mary...

The grace of our Lord Jesus Christ, and the love of God, and the communion of the Holy Spirit be with you all. Amen. (2 Cor 13:13)
Hail Mary...

Grace and peace to you from God the Father, and from our Lord Jesus Christ, who gave himself on behalf of our sins, so that he might deliver us from this present wicked age, according to the will of God our Father. (Gal 1:3-4)
Hail Mary...

When it pleased God who had set me apart from before I was born, and who has called me by his grace, to reveal his Son to me, so that I might evangelize him among the Gentiles. (Gal 1:15-16)
Hail Mary...

Though I live now in the flesh, I live in the faith of the Son of God, who loved me and who delivered himself for me. (Gal 2:20)
Hail Mary...

Christ has redeemed us from the curse of the law, since he became a curse for us. For it is written: "Cursed is anyone who hangs from a tree." (Gal 3:13)
Hail Mary...

Now that faith has arrived, we are no longer under a guardian. For we are all children of God, through the faith which is in Christ Jesus. (Gal 3:25-26)
Hail Mary...

Glory Be…

Decade 4

Our Father…

For as many of you as have been baptized in Christ have become clothed with Christ. (Gal 3:27)
Hail Mary...

There is neither Jew nor Greek; there is neither servant nor free; there is neither male nor female. For you are all one in Christ Jesus. (Gal 3:28)
Hail Mary...

When the fullness of time arrived, God sent his Son, formed from a woman, formed under the law, so that he might redeem those who were under the law, in order that we might receive adoption as children. (Gal 4:4-5)
Hail Mary...

Therefore, because you are children, God has sent the Spirit of his Son into your hearts, crying out: "Abba, Father." (Gal 4:6)
Hail Mary...

So you are no longer a servant, but a child. and if a child, then also an heir, through God. (Gal 4:7)
Hail Mary...

For freedom Christ has set us free. Stand firm, therefore, and do not submit again to a yoke of slavery. (Gal 5:1)
Hail Mary...

For in Christ Jesus, neither circumcision nor uncircumcision prevails over anything, but only faith which works through love. (Gal 5:6)
Hail Mary...

For the entire law is fulfilled by one word: "You shall love your neighbor as yourself." But if you bite and devour one another, be careful that you are not consumed by one another! (Gal 5:14-15)
Hail Mary...

Walk in the spirit, and you will not fulfill the desires of the flesh. (Gal 5:16)
Hail Mary...

If you are led by the Spirit, you are not under the law. (Gal 5:18)
Hail Mary...

Glory Be...

Decade 5

Our Father...

The fruit of the Spirit is love, joy, peace, patience, kindness, gentleness, faithfulness, self-control, patience and generosity. (Gal 5:22)
Hail Mary...

Those who are Christ's have crucified their flesh, along with its passions and desires. (Gal 5:24)
Hail Mary...

If we live by the Spirit, we should also be guided by the Spirit. (Gal 5:25)
Hail Mary...

Bear one another's burdens, and so shall you fulfill the law of Christ. (Gal 6:2)
Hail Mary...

Whatever a man will have sown, that also shall he reap. For whoever sows in his flesh, from the flesh he shall also reap corruption. But whoever sows in the Spirit, from the Spirit he shall reap eternal life. (Gal 6:8)
Hail Mary...

Let us not be deficient in doing good. For in due time, we shall reap without fail. Therefore, while we have time, we should do good works toward everyone, and most of all toward those who are of the household of the faith. (Gal 6:9-10)
Hail Mary...

But far be it from me to boast, except in the cross of our Lord Jesus Christ, through which the world is crucified to me, and I to the world. (Gal 6:14)

Hail Mary...

For in Christ Jesus, neither circumcision nor uncircumcision prevails in any way, but a new creation is everything! (Gal 6:15)
Hail Mary...

Blessed be the God and Father of our Lord Jesus Christ, who has blessed us with every spiritual blessing in the heavens, in Christ, just as he chose us in him before the foundation of the world, so that we would be holy and blameless in his sight, in love. (Eph 1:3-4)
Hail Mary...

He has predestined us to adoption as children, through Jesus Christ, in himself, according to the purpose of his will, for the praise of the glory of his grace, with which he has gifted us in his beloved Son. (Eph 1:5-6)
Hail Mary...

Glory Be...

Day 26

Decade 1

Our Father…

In him, we have redemption through his blood: the remission of sins in accord with the riches of his grace. (Eph 1:7)

Hail Mary...

In him, you also, after you heard and believed the Word of truth, which is the Gospel of your salvation, were sealed with the promise of the Holy Spirit. (Eph 1:13)

Hail Mary...

I pray that the God of our Lord Jesus Christ, the Father of glory, may give a spirit of wisdom and of revelation to you, as you come to know him. (Eph 1:17)

Hail Mary...

God put this power to work in Christ, raising him from the dead and establishing him at his right hand in the heavens, above every principality and power and virtue and dominion, and above every name that is given, not only in this age, but even in the age to come. (Eph 1:20-21)

Hail Mary...

He has subjected all things under his feet, and he has made him the head over the entire Church, which is his body, the fullness of him who accomplishes everything in everyone. (Eph 1:22-23)

Hail Mary...

God, who is rich in mercy, for the sake of his exceedingly great love with which he loved us, even when we were dead in our sins, has enlivened us together in Christ, by whose grace you have been saved. (Eph 2:4-5)

Hail Mary...

For by grace, you have been saved through faith. And this is not your doing, for it is a gift of God. (Eph 2:8)

Hail Mary...

For we are his handiwork, created in Christ Jesus for the good works which God has prepared and in which we should walk. (Eph 2:10)

Hail Mary...

In Christ Jesus, you, who were in times past far away, have been brought near by the blood of Christ. (Eph 2:13)

Hail Mary...

Now, therefore, you are no longer strangers and aliens. Instead, you are citizens among the saints in the household of God, having been built upon the foundation of the Apostles and of the Prophets, with Jesus Christ himself as the cornerstone. (Eph 2:19-20)
Hail Mary...

Glory Be…

Decade 2
Our Father…

In him, all that has been built is framed together, rising up into a holy temple in the Lord. In him, you also have been built together into a dwelling place for God in the Spirit. (Eph 2:21-22)
Hail Mary...

I pray that he would grant you, according to the riches of his glory, to be strengthened with power by his Spirit in your inner being. (Eph 3:16)
Hail Mary...

I pray that you be able to embrace, with all the saints, what is the width and length and height and depth of the love of Christ, and even be able to know that which surpasses all knowledge, so that you may be filled with all the fullness of God. (Eph 3:18-19)
Hail Mary...

Now to him who by the power that is at work within us, is able to do all things, more abundantly than we could ever ask or imagine, to him be glory, in the Church and in Christ Jesus, throughout every generation, forever and ever. (Eph 3:20-21)
Hail Mary...

One body and one Spirit: to this you have been called by the one hope of your calling: one Lord, one faith, one baptism, one God and Father of all, who is over all, and through all, and in us all. (Eph 4:4-6)
Hail Mary...

We should increase in everything, in him who is the head, Christ himself. For in him, the whole body is joined closely together, by every underlying joint, through the function allotted to each part, bringing growth to the body, toward its edification in love. (Eph 4:15-16)
Hail Mary...

You were taught to set aside your earlier behavior, the former man, who was corrupted, by means of desire, unto error, and so be renewed in the spirit of

your mind, and so put on the new man, who, in accord with God, is created in justice and in the holiness of truth. (Eph 4:22-24)
Hail Mary...

Let no evil words proceed from your mouth, but only what is good, toward the edification of faith, so as to bestow grace upon those who listen. (Eph 4:29)
Hail Mary...

Do not be willing to grieve the Holy Spirit of God, in whom you have been sealed, unto the day of redemption. (Eph 4:30)
Hail Mary...

Be kind and merciful to one another, forgiving one another, just as God has forgiven you in Christ. (Eph 4:32)
Hail Mary...

Glory Be...

Decade 3
Our Father...

Therefore, as beloved children, be imitators of God. Walk in love, just as Christ also loved us and delivered himself for us, as a fragrant offering and a sacrifice to God. (Eph 5:1-2)
Hail Mary...

For you were darkness, in times past, but now you are light, in the Lord. So then, walk as children of the light. (Eph 5:8)
Hail Mary...

Do not choose to be drunk with wine, for this is self-indulgence. Instead, be filled with the Holy Spirit, speaking among yourselves in psalms and hymns and spiritual canticles, singing and reciting psalms to the Lord in your hearts, giving thanks to God the father always and for everything, in the name of our Lord Jesus Christ. (Eph 5:18-20)
Hail Mary...

No man has ever hated his own flesh, but instead he nourishes and cherishes it, as Christ also does to the Church. For we are a part of his body, of his flesh and of his bones. (Eph 5:29-30)
Hail Mary...

Children, obey your parents in the Lord, for this is right. Honor your father and your mother. This is the first commandment with a promise: so that it may be well with you, and so that you may have a long life upon the earth. (Eph 6:1-3)

Hail Mary...

Serve with good will, as to the Lord, and not to men. For you know that whatever good we will do, we will receive the same again from the Lord. (Eph 6:7-8)
Hail Mary...

Be strong in the Lord, and in the power of his might. (Eph 6:10)
Hail Mary...

Put on the whole armor of God, so that you may be able to stand against the wiles of the devil. (Eph 6:11)
Hail Mary...

We wrestle not against flesh and blood, but against principalities, against powers, against the rulers of the darkness of this world, against spiritual wickedness in high places. Therefore take unto you the whole armor of God, so that you may be able to withstand in the evil day, and having done everything, to stand firm. (Eph 6:12-13)
Hail Mary...

Stand therefore, having your loins girded with the belt of truth, and put on the breastplate of righteousness; And for your feet put on whatever will prepare you for the proclamation of the gospel of peace; Above all, taking the shield of faith, with which you shall be able to quench all the fiery darts of the wicked. And take the helmet of salvation, and the sword of the Spirit, which is the word of God. (Eph 6:14-17)
Hail Mary...

Glory Be…

Decade 4
Our Father…

Pray in the Spirit at all times in every prayer and supplication. (Eph 6:18)
Hail Mary...

I am confident of this very thing: that he who has begun this good work in you will bring it to completion, by the day of Christ Jesus. (Phil 1:6)
Hail Mary...

This has been given to you on behalf of Christ, not only so that you may believe in him, but even so that you may suffer with him, engaging in the same struggle, of a kind which you also have seen in me, and which you now have heard from me. (Phil 1:29-30)
Hail Mary...

God has also exalted him and has given him a name which is above every name, so that, at the name of Jesus, every knee should bend, in heaven and on earth and under the earth, and so that every tongue should confess that Jesus Christ is Lord, to the glory of God the Father. (Phil 2:9-11)
Hail Mary...

Look upon what he has done for us, and, with fear and trembling, acknowledge him. (Phil 2:12)
Hail Mary...

Do everything without murmuring or hesitation. So may you be without blame, innocent children of God, without reproof, in the midst of a depraved and perverse nation, among whom you shine like stars in the world. (Phil 2:14-15)
Hail Mary...

It is by holding fast to the Word of Life that I can glory in the day of Christ that I have not run in vain, nor have I labored in vain. (Phil 2:16)
Hail Mary...

I consider everything to be a loss, because of the surpassing value of knowing Jesus Christ, my Lord, for whose sake I have suffered the loss of everything, considering it all to be like rubbish, so that I may gain Christ. (Phil 3:8-9)
Hail Mary...

I do not consider that I have already attained this. Instead, I do one thing: forgetting those things that are behind, and straining forward toward those things that lie ahead, I pursue the goal, the prize of the heavenly calling of God in Christ Jesus. (Phil 3:13-14)
Hail Mary...

Our way of life is in heaven. And from heaven, too, we await the Savior, our Lord Jesus Christ, who will transform the body of our lowliness that it may be conformed to his glorious body, by means of that power by which he is able to subject all things to himself. (Phil 3:20-21)
Hail Mary...

Glory Be...

Decade 5

Our Father...

Rejoice in the Lord always. Again, I say, rejoice. (Phil 4:4)
Hail Mary...

Let your gentleness be known to all men. The Lord is near. (Phil 4:5)
Hail Mary...

Be anxious about nothing. But in all things, with prayer and supplication, with acts of thanksgiving, let your petitions be made known to God. (Phil 4:6)
Hail Mary...

The peace of God, which surpasses all understanding, shall keep your hearts and minds through Christ Jesus. (Phil 4:7)
Hail Mary...

Whatever is true, whatever is chaste, whatever is just, whatever is holy, whatever is worthy to be loved, whatever is of good repute, if there is any virtue, if there is anything worthy of praise: meditate on these. (Phil 4:8)
Hail Mary...

I can do all things in him who strengthens me. (Phil 4:13)
Hail Mary...

My God shall supply all your needs according to his riches in glory by Christ Jesus. (Phil 4:19)
Hail Mary...

Being strengthened with all the strength, in accord with the power of his glory, may you be prepared to endure everything with all patience, with joy, giving thanks to God the Father, who has made us worthy to have a share in the inheritance of the saints in the light. (Col 1:11-12)
Hail Mary...

He has rescued us from the power of darkness, and he has transferred us into the kingdom of his beloved son, in whom we have redemption, the forgiveness of sins. (Col 1:13-14)
Hail Mary...

For in him was created everything in heaven and on earth, visible and invisible, whether thrones, or dominations, or principalities, or powers. All things were created through him and in him and he is before all, and in him all things hold together. (Col 1:16-17)
Hail Mary...

Glory Be…

Day 27

Decade 1

Our Father…

He is the head of his body, the Church. He is the beginning, the first-born from the dead, so that in all things he may hold first place in everything. (Col 1:18)

Hail Mary...

The Father is well-pleased that all fullness reside in him, and that, through him, all things be reconciled to himself, making peace through the blood of his cross, for the things that are on earth, as well as the things that are in heaven. (Col 1:19-20)

Hail Mary...

I am now rejoicing in my suffering on your behalf, and I am completing in my flesh the things that are lacking in the Passion of Christ, for the sake of his body, which is the Church. (Col 1:24)

Hail Mary...

You have been buried with him in baptism. In him also, you have risen again through faith, by the work of God, who raised him up from the dead. (Col 2:12)

Hail Mary...

Be rooted and continually built up in Christ. And be confirmed in the faith, just as you have also learned it, increasing in him with acts of thanksgiving.. (Col 2:7)

Hail Mary...

In him, all the fullness of the divine nature dwells bodily and in him, you have been filled; for he is the head of all principality and power. (Col 2:9-10)

Hail Mary...

When you were dead in your transgressions and in the uncircumcision of your flesh, he enlivened you, together with him, forgiving us of all transgressions and erasing the record that stood against us with its legal demands. He has taken this away from our midst, nailing it to the Cross. (Col 2:13-14)

Hail Mary...

You have died, and so your life is hidden with Christ in God. (Col 3:3)

Hail Mary...

Strip yourselves of the old man, with his deeds, and clothe yourself with the new man, who has been renewed by knowledge, in accord with the image of the One who created him. (Col 3:9-10)
Hail Mary...

You are the people of God, holy and beloved, therefore, clothe yourselves with compassion, kindness, humility, modesty, and patience. (Col 3:12)
Hail Mary...

Glory Be...

Decade 2

Our Father...

Bear with one another, and, if anyone has a complaint against another, forgive one another. For just as the Lord has forgiven you, so also must you do. Above all these things put on love, which is the bond of perfection. (Col 3:13-14)
Hail Mary...

Let the peace of Christ lift up your hearts. For in this peace, you have been called, as one body. (Col 3:15)
Hail Mary...

Let the word of Christ live in you in abundance, with all wisdom, teaching and correcting one another, with Psalms, hymns, and spiritual songs, singing to God with gratitude in your hearts. (Col 3:16)
Hail Mary...

Let everything whatsoever that you do, whether in word or in deed, be done all in the name of the Lord Jesus Christ, giving thanks to God the Father through him. (Col 3:17)
Hail Mary...

Children, obey your parents in all things. For this is well-pleasing to the Lord. (Col 3:20)
Hail Mary...

Whatever your task, do it from the heart, as done for the Lord, and not for men. For you know that you will receive from the Lord the repayment of an inheritance. (Col 3:23-24)
Hail Mary...

Devote yourselves in prayer. Be watchful in prayer with acts of thanksgiving. (Col 4:2)
Hail Mary...

Our Gospel has not been among you in word alone, but also in power, and in the Holy Spirit, and with full conviction. (1 Thes 1:5)
Hail Mary...

We give thanks to God without ceasing: because, when you had accepted from us the Word of God, you accepted it not as a human word, but as it truly is, God's Word, which is at work in you who have believed. (1 Thes 2:13)
Hail Mary...

God has not called us to impurity, but to sanctification. (1 Thes 4:7)
Hail Mary...

Glory Be…

Decade 3
Our Father…

If we believe that Jesus has died and risen again, even so, through Jesus, God bring back with him those who have died. (1 Thes 4:14)
Hail Mary...

For the Lord himself, with a command and with the voice of an Archangel and with a trumpet of God, shall descend from heaven. And the dead, who are in Christ, shall rise up first. Next, we who are alive, who are remaining, shall be taken up quickly together with them into the clouds to meet Christ in the air. And in this way, we shall be with the Lord always. (1 Thes 4:16-17)
Hail Mary...

You yourselves thoroughly understand that the day of the Lord shall arrive much like a thief in the night. For when they will say, "Peace and security!" then destruction will suddenly overwhelm them, like the labor pains of a woman with child, and they will not escape. (1 Thes 5:2-3)
Hail Mary...

For all of you are children of light and children of the day; we are not of the night, nor of darkness. Therefore, let us not sleep, as the rest do. Instead, we should be vigilant and sober. (1 Thes 5:5-6)
Hail Mary...

Rejoice always. Pray without ceasing. Give thanks in everything. For this is the will of God in Christ Jesus for all of you. (1 Thes 5:16-18)
Hail Mary...

May the God of peace himself sanctify you through all things, so that your whole spirit and soul and body may be preserved without blame unto the return of our Lord Jesus Christ. (1 Thes 5:23)
Hail Mary...

We pray always for you, so that our God may make you worthy of his calling and may fulfill by his power every act of his goodness as well as his work of faith, in order that the name of our Lord Jesus may be glorified in you, and you in him, in accord with the grace of our God and of the Lord Jesus Christ. (2 Thes 1:11-12)
Hail Mary...

Brothers, stand firm, and hold to the traditions that you have learned, whether by word or by our letter. (2 Thes 2:15)
Hail Mary...

May our Lord Jesus Christ himself, and God our Father, who has loved us and who has given us an everlasting consolation and good hope in grace, comfort your hearts and strengthen them in every good word and deed. (2 Thes 2:16-17)
Hail Mary...

God is faithful. He will strengthen you, and he will guard you from the evil one. (2 Thes 3:3)
Hail Mary...

Glory Be…

Decade 4
Our Father…

May the Lord direct your hearts, in the love of God and with the patience of Christ. (2 Thes 3:5)
Hail Mary...

May the Lord of peace himself give you an everlasting peace, in all ways. May the Lord be with all of you. (2 Thes 3:16)
Hail Mary...

May the grace of our Lord Jesus Christ be with you all. (2 Thes 3:18)
Hail Mary...

I give thanks to him who has strengthened me, Christ Jesus our Lord, because he has considered me faithful and appointed me to his service. (1 Tim 1:12)
Hail Mary...

It is a faithful saying, and worthy of acceptance by everyone, that Christ Jesus came into this world to bring salvation to sinners, among whom I am the foremost. (1 Tim 1:15)
Hail Mary...

It was for this reason that I obtained mercy, so that in me as first, Christ Jesus would display all patience, for the instruction of those who would believe in him unto eternal life. (1 Tim 1:16)
Hail Mary...

There is one God, and one mediator of God and of men, the man Christ Jesus, who gave himself as a redemption for all, as a testimony in its proper time. (1 Tim 2:5-6)
Hail Mary...

Everything created by God is good, and nothing is to be rejected which is received with thanksgiving; for it has been sanctified by the Word of God and by prayer. (1 Tim 4:4-5)
Hail Mary...

For the exercise of the body is somewhat useful. But piety is useful in all things, holding the promise of life for both the present and for the future to come. (1 Tim 4:8)
Hail Mary...

Do not neglect the gift that is within you, which was given to you through prophecy, with the laying on of the hands by the council of elders. Meditate on these things, so that your progress may be manifest to all. (1 Tim 4:14-15)
Hail Mary...

Glory Be...

Decade 5
Our Father...

Pay attention to yourself and to doctrine. Pursue these things. For in doing so, you will save both yourself and those who listen to you. (1 Tim 4:16)
Hail Mary...

Godliness with contentment is great gain. For we brought nothing into this world, and there is no doubt that we can take nothing away. But, having food and clothing, we should be content with these. (1 Tim 6:6-8)
Hail Mary...

Those who want to become rich fall into temptation and into the snare of the devil and into many useless and harmful desires, which plunge people in destruction and ruin. The love of money is the root of all evil. Some persons,

in their eagerness to be rich, have strayed from the faith and have entangled themselves in many sorrows. (1 Tim 6:9-10)
Hail Mary...

It is he alone who holds immortality, and who inhabits in unapproachable light, whom no man has seen, nor even is able to see, to whom is honor and everlasting dominion. (1 Tim 6:16)
Hail Mary...

Instruct the wealthy of this age not to have a superior attitude, nor to hope in the uncertainty of riches, but in the living God, who offers us everything in abundance to enjoy. (1 Tim 6:17)
Hail Mary...

God has not given us a spirit of cowardice, but of power, and of love, and of a sound mind. (2 Tim 1:7)
Hail Mary...

Do not be ashamed of the testimony of our Lord, nor of me, his prisoner. Instead, join with me in suffering for the Gospel with the strength that comes from God, who has freed us and has called us to his holy vocation, not according to our works, but according to his own purpose and grace, which was given to us in Christ Jesus, before the ages began. (2 Tim 1:8-9)
Hail Mary...

Labor in suffering like a good soldier of Christ Jesus. No man, acting as a soldier for God, entangles himself in every day matters, so that he may please him who enlisted him as a soldier. . (2 Tim 2:3-4)
Hail Mary...

If we are unfaithful, he remains faithful: for he cannot deny himself. (2 Tim 2:13)
Hail Mary...

If anyone, then, will have cleansed himself from these things, he shall be a vessel held in honor, sanctified and useful to the Lord, prepared for every good work. (2 Tim 2:21)
Hail Mary...

Glory Be…

Day 28

Decade 1

Our Father…

All Scripture, having been divinely inspired, is useful for teaching, for reproof, for correction, and for instruction in justice, so that the man of God may be perfect, having been trained for every good work. (2 Tim 3:16-17)

Hail Mary...

A crown of justice has been reserved for me, one which the Lord, the just judge, will render to me in that day, and not only to me, but also to those who look forward to his return. (2 Tim 4:8)

Hail Mary...

The Lord has freed me from every evil attack, and he will accomplish salvation by his heavenly kingdom. To him be glory forever and ever. Amen. (2 Tim 4:18)

Hail Mary...

For the grace of God our Savior has appeared to all men, instructing us to reject impiety and worldly desires, so that we may live soberly and justly and piously in this age, looking forward to the blessed hope and the advent of the glory of the great God and of our Savior Jesus Christ. (Tit 2:11-13)

Hail Mary...

He saved us, not by works of justice that we had done, but, in accord with his mercy, by the water of rebirth and by the renewal of the Holy Spirit. (Tit 3:5)

Hail Mary...

This Spirit, he has poured out upon us in abundance, through Jesus Christ our Savior, so that, having been justified by his grace, we may become heirs according to the hope of eternal life. (Tit 3:6-7)

Hail Mary...

In many places and in many ways, in past times, God spoke to the fathers through the Prophets; lastly, in these days, he has spoken to us through the Son. (Heb 1:1-2)

Hail Mary...

The Son is the reflection of God's glory, and the imprint of God's very being, and is carrying all things by the Word of his virtue, thereby accomplishing a purging of sins, he sits at the right hand of Majesty on high. And having been

made so much better than the Angels, he has inherited a name so much greater than theirs. (Heb 1:3-4)
Hail Mary...

In the beginning, O Lord, you founded the earth. And the heavens are the work of your hands. These shall pass away, but you will remain. And all will grow old like a garment. And you will change them like clothing, and they shall be changed. Yet you are ever the same, and your years will not diminish. (Heb 1:10-12)
Hail Mary...

Are not all angels spirits in the divine service, sent to minister for the sake of those who shall receive the inheritance of salvation? (Heb 1:14)
Hail Mary...Glory Be...

Decade 2

Our Father...

What are human beings that you are mindful of them, or mortals, that you care for him? You have reduced them to a little less than the angels. You have crowned them with glory and honor, and you have set them over the works of your hands. (Heb 2:6-7)
Hail Mary...

We understand that Jesus, who was reduced to a little less than the Angels, was crowned with glory and honor because of his Passion and death, in order that, by the grace of God, he might taste death for all. (Heb 2:9)
Hail Mary...

It was fitting for him, because of whom and through whom all things exist, who had led many children into glory, should make the pioneer of their salvation perfect through sufferings. (Heb 2:10)
Hail Mary...

He who sanctifies, and those who are sanctified, are all from One. For this reason, he is not ashamed to call them brothers, saying: "I will announce your name to my brothers. In the midst of the Church, I will praise you." (Heb 2:11-12)
Hail Mary...

Because children share flesh and blood, he himself also, in like manner, has shared in the same human nature, so that through death, he might destroy him who held the dominion of death, that is, the devil, and so that he might free those who, through the fear of death, had been condemned to be held in slavery throughout their entire life. (Heb 2:14-15)
Hail Mary...

Therefore, it is fitting for him to be made similar to his brothers in all things, so that he might become a merciful and faithful High Priest before God, in order that he might bring forgiveness to the sins of the people. (Heb 2:17)
Hail Mary...

For in as much as he himself has suffered and has been tempted, he also is able to help those who are tempted. (Heb 2:18)
Hail Mary...

Be cautious, brothers, lest perhaps there may be, in any of you, an evil heart of unbelief, turning aside from the living God. Instead, exhort one another every day, while it is still called 'today,' so that none of you may become hardened through the falseness of sin. (Heb 3:12-13)
Hail Mary...

The Word of God is living and effective: more piercing than any two edged sword, reaching to the division even between the soul and the spirit, even between the joints and the marrow, and so it discerns the thoughts and intentions of the heart. (Heb 4:12)
Hail Mary...

We do not have a high priest who is unable to have compassion on our weaknesses, but rather one who was tempted in all things, just as we are, yet without sin. (Heb 4:15)
Hail Mary...Glory Be...

Decade 3
Our Father...

Therefore, let us go forth with confidence toward the throne of grace, so that we may obtain mercy, and find grace, in a time of need. (Heb 4:16)
Hail Mary...

Although, certainly, he is the Son of God, he learned obedience by the things that he suffered. And having reached perfection, he was made the source of eternal salvation., for all who are obedient to him. (Heb 5:8-9)
Hail Mary...

God is not unjust, such that he would forget your work and the love that you have shown in his name. For you have ministered, and you continue to minister, to the saints. (Heb 6:10)
Hail Mary...

Yet we desire that each one of you display the same solicitude toward the fulfillment of hope, even unto the end, so that you may not be slow to act, but instead may be imitators of those who, through faith and patience, shall inherit the promises. (Heb 6:11-12)

Hail Mary...

This man, because he continues forever, has an everlasting priesthood. And for this reason, he is able, continuously, to save those who approach God through him, since he is ever alive to make intercession on our behalf. (Heb 7:24-25)
Hail Mary...

I will forgive their iniquities, and I will no longer remember their sins. (Heb 8:12)
Hail Mary...

If the blood of goats and oxen, and the ashes of a calf, when these are sprinkled, sanctify those who have been defiled, in order to cleanse the flesh, how much more will the blood of Christ, who through the eternal Spirit has offered himself, immaculate, to God, cleanse our conscience from dead works, in order to serve the living God? (Heb 9:13-14)
Hail Mary...

Jesus did not enter the sanctuary made with human hands, mere examples of the true things, but he entered into Heaven itself, so that he may appear now before the face of God for us.(Heb 9:24)
Hail Mary...

As it has been appointed for mortals to die one time, and after this, to be judged, so also Christ was offered, one time, in order to bear the sins of many. (Heb 9:27)
Hail Mary...

Christ who was offered once to bear the sins of many, shall appear a second time, not to take away sin, but to bring salvation to those who are eagerly waiting for him. (Heb 9:28)
Hail Mary...Glory Be…

Decade 4

Our Father…

This man, offering one sacrifice for sins, sits at the right hand of God forever, awaiting that time when his enemies will be made his footstool. (Heb 10:12-13)
Hail Mary...

This is the testament which I will commit to them after those days, says the Lord. I will instill my laws in their hearts, and I will inscribe my laws on their minds. (Heb 10:16)
Hail Mary...

I will remember their sins and their lawless deeds no more. (Heb 10:17)
Hail Mary...

Let us draw near with a true heart, in the fullness of faith, having hearts cleansed from an evil conscience, and bodies cleansed with clean water. Let us hold fast to the confession of our hope, without wavering, for he who has promised is faithful. (Heb 10:22-23)
Hail Mary...

Do not lose your confidence, which has a great reward. For it is necessary for you to be patient, so that, by doing the will of God, you may receive the promise. (Heb 10:35-36)
Hail Mary...

Faith is the substance of things hoped for, the evidence of things not seen. (Heb 11:1)
Hail Mary...

By faith, we understand the world to be fashioned by the Word of God, so that the visible might be made by the invisible. (Heb 11:3)
Hail Mary...

Without faith, it is impossible to please God. For whoever approaches God must believe that he exists, and that he rewards those who seek him. (Heb 11:6)
Hail Mary...

By faith, Abraham, when he was tested, offered Isaac, so that he who had received the promises was offering up his only son. (Heb 11:17)
Hail Mary...

Furthermore, since we are surrounded by so great a cloud of witnesses, let us set aside every burden and sin which may cling to us, and run with perseverance the race that is set before us. (Heb 12:1)
Hail Mary...Glory Be…

Decade 5

Our Father…

Let us gaze upon Jesus, as the Author and the completion of our faith, who, for the sake of the joy laid out before him, endured the cross, disregarding its shame, and who now sits at the right hand of the throne of God. (Heb 12:2)
Hail Mary...

Do not be willing to neglect the discipline of the Lord. Neither should you become weary, while being rebuked by him. For whomever the Lord loves, he chastises. And every son whom he accepts, he scourges. (Heb 12:5-6)
Hail Mary...

Persevere in discipline. God is treating you as children. But what child is there, whom his father does not correct? But if you are without that discipline in which all have become sharers, then you are illegitimate, and you are not his children. (Heb 12:7-8)
Hail Mary...

We have certainly had the fathers of our flesh as instructors, and we reverenced them. Should we not obey the Father of spirits all the more, and so live? (Heb 12:9)
Hail Mary...

Human parents, according to what seemed best to them, disciplined us for a short time: but he disciplines us for our good, that we might share his holiness. (Heb 12:10)
Hail Mary...

Now every discipline, in the present time, does not seem a gladness, of course, but a grief. But afterwards, it will repay a most peaceful fruit of righteousness to those who become trained in it. (Heb 12:11)
Hail Mary...

Lift up your drooping hands and your lax knees, and straighten the path of your feet, so that no one, being lame, may wander astray, but instead may be healed. (Heb 12:13)
Hail Mary...

Pursue peace with everyone. Pursue holiness, without which no one shall see God. (Heb 12:14)
Hail Mary...

Be contemplative, lest anyone lack the grace of God, lest any root of bitterness spring up and impede you, and by it, many might be defiled. (Heb 12:15)
Hail Mary...

Since we are receiving an immoveable kingdom, let us give thanks, by which we offer to God an acceptable worship with fear and reverence. (Heb 12:28-29)
Hail Mary...

Glory Be...

Day 29

Decade 1

Our Father…

Do not be willing to forget hospitality. For by it, certain persons, without realizing it, have received Angels as guests. Remember those who are prisoners, just as if you were imprisoned with them, and those who endure hardships, just as if you were in their place. (Heb 13:2-3)

Hail Mary...

Keep your lives free from the love of money; be content with what you have. For he himself has said, "I will not leave you, and I will not abandon you." (Heb 13:5)

Hail Mary...

The Lord is my helper. I will not fear what man can do to me. (Heb 13:6)

Hail Mary...

Through him, let us offer the sacrifice of continual praise to God, which is the fruit of lips confessing his name. (Heb 13:15)

Hail Mary...

Do not be willing to forget good works and share what you have. Such sacrifices are pleasing to the Lord. (Heb 13:16)

Hail Mary...

My brothers, when you have fallen into various trials, consider everything a joy, knowing that the testing of your faith produces endurance, and endurance brings a work to perfection, so that you may be mature and whole, deficient in nothing.(Jas 1:2-4)

Hail Mary...

If anyone among you is in need of wisdom, let him ask God, who gives abundantly to all without reproach, and it shall be given to him. (Jas 1:5)

Hail Mary...

Blessed is the man who suffers temptation. For when he has been proven, he shall receive the crown of life which God has promised to those who love him. (Jas 1:12)

Hail Mary...

No one should say, when he is tempted, that he was tempted by God. For God cannot be tempted by evil and he himself tempts no one. (Jas 1:13)

Hail Mary...

Every excellent gift and every perfect gift is from above, descending from the Father of lights, with whom there is no change, nor any shadow of turning. (Jas 1:17)
Hail Mary...

Glory Be...

Decade 2

Our Father...

You know this, my most beloved brothers. So let every man be quick to listen, but slow to speak and slow to anger; for your anger does not produce God's righteousness. (Jas 1:19-20)
Hail Mary...

Having cast away all uncleanness and an abundance of wickedness, receive with meekness the implanted Word, which is able to save your souls. (Jas 1:21)
Hail Mary...

He who gazes upon the perfect law of liberty, and who remains in it, is not a forgetful hearer, but instead a doer of the work. He shall be blessed in what he does. (Jas 1:25)
Hail Mary...

Religion that is pure and undefiled before God, the Father, is this: to care for orphans and widows in their distress, and to keep oneself unstained by the world. (Jas 1:27, NRSCVE)
Hail Mary...

If you perfect the regal law, according to the Scriptures, "You shall love your neighbor as yourself," then you do well. (Jas 2:8)
Hail Mary...

Just as the body without the spirit is dead, so also faith without works is dead. (Jas 2:26)
Hail Mary...

Submit yourselves to God. Resist the devil, and he will flee from you. Draw near to God, and he will draw near to you. (Jas 4:7- 8)
Hail Mary...

Be humbled in the sight of the Lord, and he will exalt you. (Jas 4:10)
Hail Mary...

But if you judge the law, you are not a doer of the law, but a judge. There is one lawgiver and one judge. He is able to destroy, and he is able to set free. (Jas 4:11-12)
Hail Mary...

Therefore, be patient, brothers, until the coming of the Lord. Consider that the farmer anticipates the precious fruit of the earth, waiting patiently, until he receives the early and the late rains. Therefore, you too should be patient and should strengthen your hearts. For the coming of the Lord draws near. (Jas 5:7-8)
Hail Mary...

Glory Be...

Decade 3

Our Father...

Brothers, do not complain against one another, so that you may not be judged. Behold, the judge stands before the door. (Jas 5:9)
Hail Mary...

My brothers, consider the Prophets, who spoke in the name of the Lord, as an example of suffering, and of patience. We call them blessed those who have endured. You have heard of the patient suffering of Job. And you have seen the purpose of the Lord, that the Lord is merciful and compassionate. (Jas 5:10-11)
Hail Mary...

Before all things, my brothers, do not choose to swear, neither by heaven, nor by the earth, nor in any other oath. But let your word 'Yes' be yes, and your word 'No' be no, so that you may not fall under judgment. (Jas 5:12)
Hail Mary...

Is any of you sad? Let him pray. Is any cheerful? Let him sing psalms of praise. (Jas 5:13)
Hail Mary...

Is anyone ill among you? Let him bring in the priests of the Church, and let them pray over him, anointing him with oil in the name of the Lord. (Jas 5:14)
Hail Mary...

Prayer made in faith will heal the sick; the Lord will restore them to health, and the sins they have committed will be forgiven. (Jas 5:15)
Hail Mary...

Confess your sins to one another, and pray for one another, so that you may be healed. The prayer of the righteous is powerful and effective. (Jas 5:16)

Hail Mary...

If anyone of you strays from the truth, and if someone converts him, he ought to know that whoever causes a sinner to be converted from the error of his ways will save his soul from death and will cover a multitude of sins. (Jas 5:19-20)
Hail Mary...

Blessed be the God and Father of our Lord Jesus Christ, who according to his great mercy has regenerated us into a living hope, through the resurrection of Jesus Christ from the dead: unto an incorruptible and undefiled and unfading inheritance, which is reserved for you in heaven. (1 Pet 1:3-4)
Hail Mary...

In this, you should exult, if now, for a brief time, it is necessary to be made sorrowful by various trials, so that the testing of your faith, which is much more precious than gold tested by fire, may be found in praise and glory and honor at the revelation of Jesus Christ. (1 Pet 1:6-7)
Hail Mary...

Glory Be…

Decade 4
Our Father…

Prepare your minds for action, discipline yourselves, and set your hope perfectly in the grace that is offered to you in the revelation of Jesus Christ. (1 Pet 1:13)
Hail Mary...

As he who has called you is holy, in every conduct, you yourself must be holy, for it is written: “You shall be holy, for I am Holy.” (1 Pet 1:15-16)
Hail Mary...

For you know that it was not with corruptible gold or silver that you were redeemed away from your useless behavior in the traditions of your fathers, but it was with the precious blood of Christ, an immaculate and undefiled lamb. (1 Pet 1:18-19)
Hail Mary...

He was chosen by God, before the foundation of the world, and made manifest in these latter times for your sake. Through him, you have been faithful to God, who raised him up from the dead and gave him glory, so that your faith and hope would be in God. (1 Pet 1:20-21)
Hail Mary...

You have been born again, not from corruptible seed, but from what is incorruptible, from the Word of God, living and remaining for all eternity. (1 Pet 1:23)
Hail Mary...

All flesh is like the grass and all its glory is like the flower of the grass. The grass withers and its flower falls away. But the Word of the Lord endures for eternity. (1 Pet 1:24)
Hail Mary...

Behold, I am setting in Zion a chief cornerstone, elect, precious. And whoever will have believed in him will not be put to shame. (1 Pet 2:6)
Hail Mary...

You are a chosen generation, a royal priesthood, a holy nation, an acquired people, so that you may proclaim the mighty acts of him who has called you out of darkness into his marvelous light. (1 Pet 2:9)
Hail Mary...

Keep your behavior among the Gentiles to what is good, so that, when they slander you as if you were evildoers, they may, by the good works that are seen in you, glorify God when he comes to judge. (1 Pet 2:12)
Hail Mary...

For this you have been called because Christ also suffered for you, leaving you an example, so that you would follow in his footsteps. (1 Pet 2:21)
Hail Mary...

Glory Be...

Decade 5
Our Father...

He himself bore our sins in his body on the cross, so that we, having died to sin, would live for righteousness. By his wounds, you have been healed. (1 Pet 2:24)
Hail Mary...

Finally, may you all be of one mind: compassionate, loving brotherhood, merciful, meek, humble, not repaying evil with evil, nor slander with slander, but, to the contrary, repaying with blessings. For to this you have been called, so that you may inherit a blessing. (1 Pet 3:8-9)
Hail Mary...

The eyes of the Lord are upon the just, and his ears are open to their prayers (1 Pet 3:12-13)
Hail Mary...

It is better to suffer for doing good, if it is the will of God, than for doing evil. (1 Pet 3:17)
Hail Mary...

Christ also died once for our sins, the Just one on behalf of the unjust, so that he might offer us to God, having died, certainly, in the flesh, but having been enlivened by the Spirit. (1 Pet 3:18)
Hail Mary...

You also are saved, in a similar manner, by baptism, not by the testimony of sordid flesh, but by the examination of a good conscience in God, through the resurrection of Jesus Christ. (1 Pet 3:21)
Hail Mary...

Since Christ has suffered in the flesh, you also should be armed with the same intention. For he who suffers in the flesh desists from sin, so that now he may live, for the remainder of his time in the flesh, not by the desires of men, but by the will of God. (1 Pet 4:1-2)
Hail Mary...

Above all things, have a constant mutual love among yourselves. For love covers a multitude of sins. (1 Pet 4:8)
Hail Mary...

Most beloved, do not be surprised in the fiery trial taking place among you to test you, as though some strange thing is happening to you. But instead, be glad that you are sharing in the sufferings of Christ, that, when his glory will be revealed, you too may rejoice with exultation. (1 Pet 4:12-13)
Hail Mary...

If you are reproached for the name of Christ, you will be blessed, because the Spirit of glory, which is the Spirit of God, rests upon you. (1 Pet 4:14)
Hail Mary...

Glory Be…

Day 30

Decade 1

Our Father…

If one of you suffers for being a Christian, he should not be ashamed. Instead, he should glorify God because he bears his name. (1 Pet 4:16)

Hail Mary...

Clothe yourself with all humility when dealing with one another, for God resists the proud, but to the humble he gives grace. (1 Pet 5:5)

Hail Mary...

Be humbled under the powerful hand of God, so that he may exalt you in the time of visitation. (1 Pet 5:6)

Hail Mary...

Cast all your anxiety upon him, for he takes care of you. (1 Pet 5:7)

Hail Mary...

Be sober and vigilant. For your adversary, the devil, is like a roaring lion, traveling around and seeking those whom he might devour. Resist him by being strong in faith. (1 Pet 5:8-9)

Hail Mary...

After a brief time of suffering, the God of all grace, who has called us to his eternal glory in Christ Jesus, will himself perfect, confirm, and establish us. (1 Pet 5:10)

Hail Mary...

God's divine power has given us everything needed for life and piety, through the knowledge of him who has called us by his own glory and goodness. (2 Pet 1:3)

Hail Mary...

Be all the more eager, so that by good works you may confirm your calling and election. For in doing these things, you will never stumble. (2 Pet 1:10)

Hail Mary...

Understand this first: that every prophecy of Scripture does not result from one's own interpretation. For prophecy was not conveyed by human will at any time. Instead, men and women moved by the Holy Spirit spoke from God. (2 Pet 1:20-21)

Hail Mary...

The Lord knows how to rescue the godly from trials. (2 Pet 2:9)
Hail Mary...

Glory Be...

Decade 2

Our Father...

The Lord is not delaying his promise, as some imagine, but he does act patiently for your sake, not wanting anyone to perish, but wanting all to come to repentance. (2 Pet 3:9)
Hail Mary...

Yet truly, in accord with his promises, we are looking forward to the new heavens and the new earth, in which justice lives. (2 Pet 3:13)
Hail Mary...

He who was from the beginning, whom we have heard, whom we have seen with our eyes, upon whom we have gazed, and whom our hands have certainly touched: He is the Word of Life. (1 Jn 1:1)
Hail Mary...

We have seen, and we testify, and we announce to you: the Eternal Life, who was with the Father, and who appeared to us. (1 Jn 1:2)
Hail Mary...

He whom we have seen and heard, we announce to you, so that you, too, may have fellowship with us, and so that our fellowship may be with the Father and with his Son Jesus Christ. (1 Jn 1:3)
Hail Mary...

This we write to you, so that you may rejoice, and so that your joy may be full. (1 Jn 1:4)
Hail Mary...

This is the announcement which we have heard from him, and which we announce to you: that God is light, and in him there is no darkness. (1 Jn 1:5)
Hail Mary...

If we walk in the light, just as he also is in the light, then we have fellowship with one another, and the blood of Jesus Christ, his Son, cleanses us from all sin. (1 Jn 1:7)
Hail Mary...

If we confess our sins, then he who is faithful and just will forgive us our sins and cleanse us from all iniquity. (1 Jn 1:9)
Hail Mary...

My little children, this I write to you, so that you may not sin. But if anyone has sinned, we have an Advocate with the Father, Jesus Christ, the Just One. (1 Jn 2:1)
Hail Mary...

Glory Be…

Decade 3

Our Father…

He is the atoning sacrifice for our sins, and not only for our sins, but also for those of the whole world. (1 Jn 2:2)
Hail Mary...

We can be sure that we have known him by this: if we observe his commandments. Whoever claims that he knows him, and yet does not keep his commandments, is a liar, and the truth is not in him. (1 Jn 2:3-4)
Hail Mary...

Whoever keeps his word, truly in him the love of God is perfected. (1 Jn 2:5)
Hail Mary...

Whoever declares himself to abide in him, ought to walk just as he himself walked. (1 Jn 2:6)
Hail Mary...

If we say that we are in the light, yet hate others, we are in the darkness to this very hour. Whoever loves his brother abides in the light, and there is no cause of offense in him. (1 Jn 2:9-10)
Hail Mary...

I am writing to you, little children, because you have known the Father. I am writing to you, young men, because you are strong, and the Word of God abides in you, and you have overcome the evil one. (1 Jn 2:14)
Hail Mary...

Do not choose to love the world, nor the things that are in the world. If anyone loves the world, the love of the Father is not in him. (1 Jn 2:15)
Hail Mary...

The world is passing away, with its desire. But whoever does the will of God abides unto eternity. (1 Jn 2:17)
Hail Mary...

As for you, let the Anointing that you have received from him abide in you. And so, you have no need of anyone to teach you. For his Anointing teaches

you about everything, and it is the truth, and it is not a lie. And just as his Anointing has taught you, abide in him. (1 Jn 2:27)
Hail Mary...

And now, little children, abide in him, so that when he appears, we may have faith, and we may not be put to shame by him at his coming. (1 Jn 2:28)
Hail Mary...

Glory Be…

Decade 4

Our Father…

See how much of love the Father has given to us, that we would be called, and would become, the children of God. Because of this, the world does not know us, for it did not know God. (1 Jn 3:1)
Hail Mary...

Most beloved, we are now the children of God. But what we shall be then has not yet appeared. We know that when he does appear, we shall be like him, for we shall see him as he is. (1 Jn 3:2)
Hail Mary...

You know that he appeared in order that he might take away our sins. For in him there is no sin. (1 Jn 3:5)
Hail Mary...

Everyone who abides in him does not sin. For whoever sins has not seen him, and has not known him. (1 Jn 3:6)
Hail Mary...

Whoever commits sin is of the devil. For the devil sins from the beginning. For this reason, the Son of God appeared, so that he might destroy the works of the devil. (1 Jn 3:8)
Hail Mary...

All those who have been born of God do not commit sin, for God's seed abides in them, and they cannot sin, because they were born of God. (1 Jn 3:9)
Hail Mary...

We know the love of God in this way: because he laid down his life for us. And so, we must lay down our lives for our brothers. (1 Jn 3:16)
Hail Mary...

Whoever possesses the goods of this world, and sees his brother to be in need, and yet closes his heart to him: in what way does the love of God abide in him? (1 Jn 3:17)
Hail Mary...

Whatever we shall request of him, we shall receive from him. For we keep his commandments, and we do the things that are pleasing in his sight. (1 Jn 3:22)
Hail Mary...

This is his commandment: that we should believe in the name of his Son, Jesus Christ, and love one another, just as he has commanded us. (1 Jn 3:23)
Hail Mary...

Glory Be...

Decade 5

Our Father...

Those who keep his commandments abide in him, and he in them. And we know that he abides in us by this: by the Spirit, whom he has given to us. (1 Jn 3:24)
Hail Mary...

Every spirit who confesses that Jesus Christ has arrived in the flesh is of God; and every spirit who contradicts Jesus is not of God. (1 Jn 4:3)
Hail Mary...

Little children, you are of God, and so you have conquered him. For he who is in you is greater than he who is in the world. (1 Jn 4:4)
Hail Mary...

Most beloved, let us love one another. For love is of God. And everyone who loves is born of God and knows God. Whoever does not love, does not know God. For God is love. (1 Jn 4:7-8)
Hail Mary...

The love of God was made apparent to us in this way: that God sent his only-begotten Son into the world, so that we might live through him. In this is love: not as if we had loved God, but that he first loved us, and so he sent his Son as a atoning sacrifice for our sins. (1 Jn 4:9-10)
Hail Mary...

Most beloved, if God has so loved us, we also ought to love one another. No one has ever seen God. But if we love one another, God abides in us, and his love is perfected in us. (1 Jn 4:11-12)
Hail Mary...

We have seen, and we testify, that the Father has sent his Son to be the Savior of the world. Whoever has confessed that Jesus is the Son of God, God abides in him, and he in God. (1 Jn 4:14-15)
Hail Mary...

God is love. And he who abides in love, abides in God, and God in him. (1 Jn 4:16)
Hail Mary...

There is no fear in love. Instead, perfect love casts out fear, for fear pertains to punishment. And whoever fears is not perfected in love. (1 Jn 4:18)
Hail Mary...

Everyone who believes that Jesus is the Christ, is born of God. (1 Jn 5:1)
Hail Mary...

Glory Be...

Day 31

Decade 1

Our Father…

This is the love of God: that we keep his commandments. And his commandments are not burdensome. (1 Jn 5:3)

Hail Mary...

All that is born of God overcomes the world. And this is the victory that overcomes the world: our faith. Who is it that overcomes the world? Only he who believes that Jesus is the Son of God! (1 Jn 5:4-5)

Hail Mary...

Whoever has the Son, has Life. Whoever does not have the Son, does not have Life. (1 Jn 5:12)

Hail Mary...

This is the boldness which we have toward God that if we ask anything according to his will, he hears us. (1 Jn 5:14)

Hail Mary...

We know that he hears us, no matter what we request; so we know that we can obtain the things that we request of him. (1 Jn 5:15)

Hail Mary...

We know that everyone who is born of God does not sin. Instead, the one who was born of God protects him, and the evil one cannot touch him. (1 Jn 5:18)

Hail Mary...

We know that the Son of God has arrived, and that he has given us understanding, so that we may know the true God, and so that we may remain in his true Son. This is the true God, and this is Eternal Life. (1 Jn 5:20)

Hail Mary...

This is love: that we walk according to his commandments. For this is the commandment that you have heard in the same way from the beginning, and in which you should walk. (2 Jn 1:6)

Hail Mary...

Everyone who does not abide in the teaching of Christ, but withdraws from it, does not have God. Whoever abides in the teaching has both the Father and the Son. (2 Jn 1:9)

Hail Mary...

Now, to him who has the power to keep you free from sin and to present you, immaculate, with exultation, before the presence of his glory at the advent of our Lord Jesus Christ, to the only God, our Savior, through Jesus Christ our Lord: to him be glory and majesty, dominion and power, before all ages, and now, and in every age, forever. Amen. (Jude 1:24-25)
Hail Mary...

Glory Be...

Decade 2
Our Father...

Blessed is they that read aloud the words of the prophecy, and they that hear the words of this prophecy, and keep those things which are written in it. (Rev 1:3)
Hail Mary...

Grace and peace to you, from him who is, and who was, and who is to come. (Rev 1:4)
Hail Mary...

Jesus Christ, who is the faithful witness, the first-born of the dead, and the leader over the kings of the earth, who has loved us and has washed us from our sins with his blood, and who has made us into a kingdom and into priests for God and for his Father. To him be glory and dominion forever and ever. (Rev 1:5-6)
Hail Mary...

Behold, he arrives with the clouds, and every eye shall see him, even those who pierced him. (Rev 1:7)
Hail Mary...

"I am the Alpha and the Omega, the Beginning and the End," says the Lord God, who is, and who was, and who is to come, the Almighty. (Rev 1:8)
Hail Mary...

When I had seen him, I fell at his feet, like one who is dead. And he laid his right hand upon me, saying: "Do not be afraid. I am the First and the Last." (Rev 1:17)
Hail Mary...

Whoever has an ear, let him hear what the Spirit says to the Churches. To him who prevails, I will give to eat from the Tree of Life, which is in the Paradise of my God. (Rev 2:7)
Hail Mary...

You should fear nothing amid those things which you will suffer. Behold, the devil will cast some of you into prison, so that you may be tested. (Rev 2:10)
Hail Mary...

Be faithful even unto death, and I will give to you the crown of life. (Rev 2:10)
Hail Mary...

Whoever prevails, I will set him as a column in the temple of my God, and he shall not depart from it anymore. And I will write upon him the name of my God, and the name of the city of my God, the new Jerusalem that descends out of heaven from my God, and my own new name. (Rev 3:12)
Hail Mary...

Glory Be...

Decade 3
Our Father...

Those whom I love, I rebuke and chastise. Therefore, be zealous and do penance. (Rev 3:19)
Hail Mary...

Behold, I stand at the door and knock. If anyone will hear my voice and will open the door to me, I will enter to him, and I will dine with him, and he with me. (Rev 3:20)
Hail Mary...

Whoever conquers, I will grant to him to sit with me on my throne, just as I also have conquered and have sat down with my Father on his throne. (Rev 3:21)
Hail Mary...

They sang a new song: O Lord, you are worthy to take the scroll and to open its seals, because you were slain and have redeemed us for God, by your blood, from every tribe and language and people and nation. (Rev 5:9)
Hail Mary...

Salvation is from our God, who sits upon the throne, and from the Lamb. (Rev 7:10)
Hail Mary...

They are before the throne of God, and they serve him, day and night, in his temple. And the One who sits upon the throne shall dwell over them. They shall not hunger, nor shall they thirst, anymore. Neither shall the sun beat down upon them, nor any heat. For the Lamb, who is in the midst of the throne, will rule over them, and he will lead them to the fountains of the

waters of life. And God will wipe away every tear from their eyes. (Rev 7:15-17)
Hail Mary...

The nations became angry, but your wrath arrived, and the time for the dead to be judged, and to render a reward to your servants the prophets, and to the saints, and to those who fear your name, small and great, and to destroy those who have corrupted the earth. (Rev 11:18)
Hail Mary...

The great dragon was thrown down, that ancient serpent, who is called the Devil and Satan, the deceiver of the whole world—he was thrown down to the earth, and his angels were thrown down with him. (Rev 12:9)
Hail Mary...

I heard a great voice in heaven, saying: "Now have arrived the salvation and the power and the kingdom of our God and the authority of his Messiah, for the accuser of our brothers has been cast down, he who accused them before our God day and night. (Rev 12:10)
Hail Mary...

They overcame him by the blood of the Lamb and by the word of his testimony. And they loved not their own lives, even unto death. (Rev 12:11)
Hail Mary...

Glory Be…

Decade 4
Our Father…

Fear the Lord, and give honor to him, for the hour of his judgment has arrived. And worship him who made heaven and earth, the sea and the springs of water. (Rev 14:7)
Hail Mary...

And I saw, and behold, a white cloud. And upon the cloud was one sitting, resembling a son of man, having a crown of gold on his head, and a sharp sickle in his hand. (Rev 14:14)
Hail Mary...

I saw something like a sea of glass mixed with fire. And those who had overcome the beast and his image and the number of his name, were standing upon the sea of glass, holding the harps of God, and singing the canticle of Moses, the servant of God, and the canticle of the Lamb. (Rev 15:2)
Hail Mary...

Great and marvelous are your works, Lord God Almighty; just and true are your ways, you King of the nations. Who shall not fear you, O Lord, and glorify your name? for you alone are holy: for all nations shall come and worship before you. (Rev 15:3-4)
Hail Mary...

These shall fight against the Lamb, and the Lamb shall conquer them. For he is the Lord of lords and the King of kings. And those who are with him are called, and chosen, and faithful. (Rev 17:14)
Hail Mary...

Let us be glad and exult. And let us give glory to him. For the marriage feast of the Lamb has arrived, and his bride has prepared herself. (Rev 19:7)
Hail Mary...

The angel said to me: "Write: Blessed are those who have been called to the wedding feast of the Lamb." And he said to me, "These are true words of God." (Rev 19:9)
Hail Mary...

He was clothed with a vestment sprinkled with blood. And his name is called: THE WORD OF GOD. (Rev 19:13)
Hail Mary...

And he apprehended the dragon, the ancient serpent, who is the devil and Satan, and he bound him for a thousand years. And he cast him into the abyss, and he closed and sealed it, so that he would no longer seduce the nations, until the thousand years are completed. (Rev 20:2-3)
Hail Mary...

I saw the dead, great and small, standing in view of the throne. And books were opened. And another Book was opened, which is the Book of Life. And the dead were judged by those things that had been written in the books, according to their works. (Rev 20:12)
Hail Mary...

Glory Be...

Decade 5
Our Father...

I saw the new heaven and the new earth. For the first heaven and the first earth passed away, and the sea is no more. And I, John, saw the Holy City, the New Jerusalem, descending out of heaven from God, prepared like a bride adorned for her husband. (Rev 21:1-2)
Hail Mary...

I heard a great voice from the throne, saying: "Behold the tabernacle of God is among mortals. He will dwell with them, and they will be his people. And God himself will be with them. (Rev 21:3)
Hail Mary...

God will wipe away every tear from their eyes. And death shall be no more. And neither mourning, nor crying out, nor grief shall be anymore. For the first things have passed away. (Rev 21:4)
Hail Mary...

I am the Alpha and the Omega, the Beginning and the End. To those who thirst, I will give freely from the fountain of the water of life. (Rev 21:6)
Hail Mary...

There shall not enter into it anything defiled, nor anything causing an abomination, nor anything false, but only those who have been written in the Book of Life of the Lamb. (Rev 21:26)
Hail Mary...

They shall see his face. And his name shall be on their foreheads. (Rev 22:4)
Hail Mary...

Night shall be no more. And they will not need the light of a lamp, nor the light of the sun, because the Lord God will be their light. And they shall reign forever and ever. (Rev 22:5)
Hail Mary...

Behold, I am approaching quickly! and my reward is with me, to render to each one according to his works. (Rev 22:12)
Hail Mary...

Blessed are those who wash their robes in the blood of the Lamb. So may they have a right to the tree of life; so may they enter through the gates into the City. (Rev 22:14)
Hail Mary...

He who offers testimony to these things, says: "Surely I am coming soon." Amen. Come, Lord Jesus. (Rev 22:20)
Hail Mary...

Glory Be…

Abbreviation

Gen-Genesis
Exo-Exodus
Lev-Leviticus
Num-Numbers
Deut-Deuteronomy
Josh-Joshua
Judg-Judges
Ruth-Ruth
1 Sam-1 Samuel
2 Sam-2 Samuel
1 Kgs-1 Kings
2 Kgs-2 Kings
1 Chron-1 Chronicles
2 Chron-2 Chronicles
Ezr-Ezra
Neh-Nehemiah
Tob-Tobith
Judith-Judith
Est-Esther
1 Mac-1 Maccabees
2 Mac-2 Maccabees
Job-Job
Ps-Psalms
Pro-Proverbs
Eccl-Ecclesiastes
Song-Song of Solomon
Wis-Wisdom
Sir-Sirach
Is- Isaiah
Jer-Jeremiah
Lam-Lamentations
Bar-Baruch
Eze-Ezekiel
Dan-Daniel
Hos-Hosea
Joel-Joel
Amos-Amos
Obad-Obadiah
Jon-Jonah
Mic-Micah
Nah-Nahum
Hab-Habakkuk
Zeph-Zephaniah
Hag-Haggai
Zech-Zechariah
Mal-Malachi
Matt-Matthew
Mrk-Mark
Luk-Luke
Jn-John
Acts-Acts
Rom-Romans
1 Cor-1 Corinthians
2 Cor-2 Corinthians
Gal-Galatians
Eph-Ephesians
Phil-Philippians
Col-Colossians
Tit-Titus
Phlm-Philemon
1 Thes-1 Thessalonians
2 Thes-2 Thessalonians
1 Tim- 1Timothy
2 Tim-2 Timothy
Heb-Hebrew
Jas-James
1 Pet-1 Peter
2 Pet-2 Peter
1 Jn- 1 John
2 Jn- 2 John
3 Jn- 3 John
Jude-Jude
Rev-Revelation

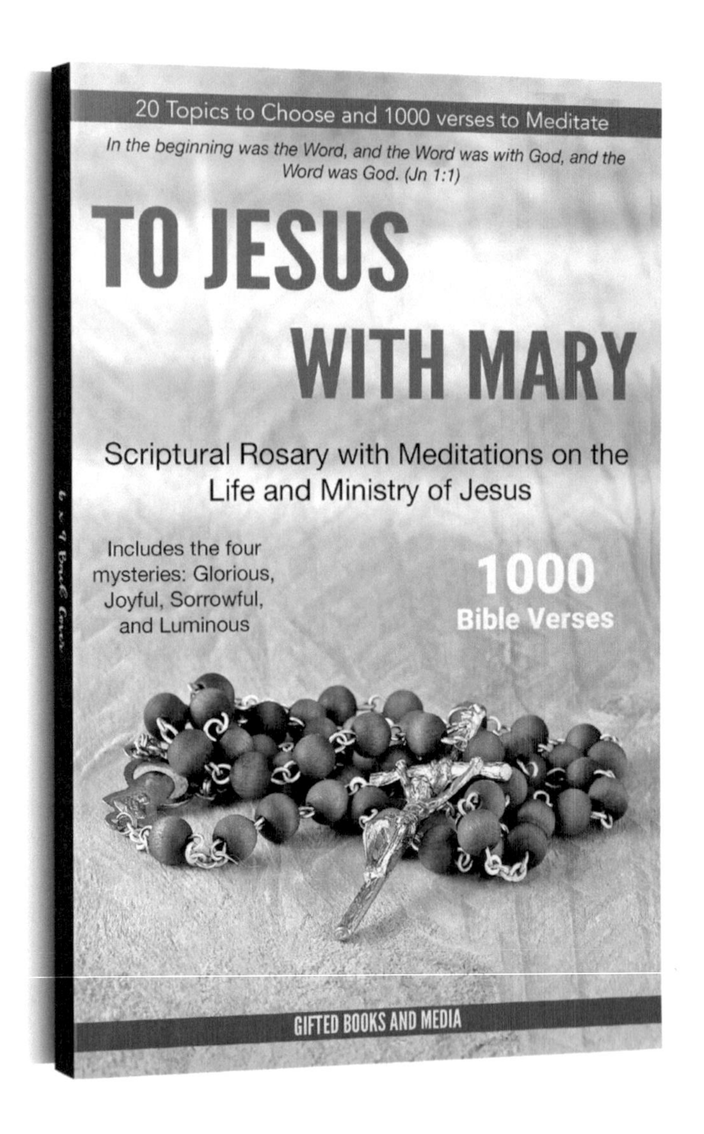
20 Topics to Choose and 1000 verses to Meditate
In the beginning was the Word, and the Word was with God, and the Word was God. (Jn 1:1)
TO JESUS
WITH MARY
Scriptural Rosary with Meditations on the Life and Ministry of Jesus
Includes the four mysteries: Glorious, Joyful, Sorrowful, and Luminous
1000
Bible Verses
GIFTED BOOKS AND MEDIA

More Titles from Gifted Books and Media

RETURN TO GOD
Confession Handbook

PREACHER'S HANDBOOK

GOD'S PROMISES AND BLESSINGS FOR AN ABUNDANT LIFE

FREEDOM FROM PORN AND MASTURBATION

30 REASONS TO GO TO CONFESSION

EXAMINATION OF CONSCIENCE
For Teens

EUCHARISTIC ADORATION
Prayers, Devotions, and Meditations

EXAMINATION OF CONSCIENCE
For Adults

SCRIPTURAL STATIONS OF THE CROSS

GODLY CHILD
Children's Guide to Catholic Living

EXAMINATION OF CONSCIENCE
For Children

TO JESUS WITH MARY
Scriptural Rosary on the Life and Ministry of Jesus

Now on Sale
Available in Paperback and Ebook
www.giftedbookstore.com

Made in the USA
Thornton, CO
12/09/23 17:20:24

d70043ef-3c22-43e4-b30f-dc2acdb55e44R01